A HIGH COUNTRY NEWS READER

GIVE AND TAKE

How the Clinton Administration's
Public Lands Offensive Transformed
the American West

Edited by Paul Larmer

HIGH COUNTRY NEWS BOOKS
PAONIA, COLORADO

GIVE AND TAKE: How the Clinton Administration's Public Lands Offensive
Transformed the American West
Edited by Paul Larmer

Publisher's Note: All of the news coverage and essays in *Give and Take* have been
previously published in *High Country News* or broadcast on Radio High Country
News. We wish to acknowledge the vital editorial contributions to this book made
by Michelle Nijhuis and Brian Erwin.

Cover design: Totaea Rendell, Kohala Designs, www.kohaladesign.com
Page design and layout: Patty Holden

This book is published on recycled stock. High Country News Books is a signatory
to the Green Press Initiative.

High Country News Books
Post Office Box 1090
Paonia, CO 81428

Library of Congress Cataloging-in-Publication Data

Give and take : the Clinton administration's public lands offensive and
the transformation of the American West / edited by Paul Larmer.
        p. cm.
Includes index.
   ISBN 0-9744485-0-8 (Paperback)
   1. Public lands—West (U.S.)—Management. 2. Land use,
Rural—Environmental aspects—West (U.S.)—Management. 3. Government
purchasing of real property—West (U.S.) 4. Government purchasing of
real property—United States. 5. National parks and reserves—West
(U.S.) 6. National monuments—West (U.S.) 7. Conservation of natural
resources—West (U.S.)—Management. 8. United States. Bureau of Land
Management. I. Title: Clinton administration's public lands offensive
and the transformation of the American West. II. Title: At head of
title: High country news reader. III. Larmer, Paul.
   HD243.W38G58 2003
   333.73'0978'09049
                                                        2003022505

International Standard Book Number (ISBN): 0-9744485-0-8

TABLE OF CONTENTS

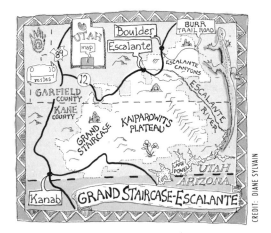

INTRODUCTION
by Paul Larmer

THERE'S SOMETHING MAGICAL about national parks and monuments in the American West. When I enter the gates of, say, Yellowstone, or Arches, or the Grand Canyon, the scenery, which had been perfectly attractive moments before, suddenly becomes stunningly beautiful. The light that illuminates the landscape, though emanating from the same sun that shown back in the city and suburbs, has a hallowed quality. It's as if I am seeing America—its forests, mountains, canyons, badlands and prairies—for the first time.

What I feel, I realize after closing my mouth and pulling off to the side of the road before crashing into something, is a sense of awe.

Part of this awesome feeling is purely physical; nationally protected places are almost by definition where the mountains are the grandest, the rivers the most untamed, the forests the deepest, the wildlife the thickest. Every smell, sound and sight informs me that these places are extraordinary.

But another part of my awe springs from the overpowering sense of history, for human intention is intertwined with every park or monument. Someone, or some group of people, had the foresight and will to set these lands aside. Who were these people, and how did they achieve their goals in the face of the powerful human drive to plough, dig, drill, log and develop every usable piece of land?

You can find some answers in the history books. The most basic tomes will tell you about John Muir, Aldo Leopold, and other pioneering conservationists, who galvanized public opinion in favor of the places they loved. The better books will also tell you that these early victories were anything but easy. There was often local opposition to the creation of national parks, and conservationists played power politics to override the angry neighbors.

The conservation of public lands remains a complex and gritty endeavor, even more so due to the growing crush of humanity looking for a place to retreat from the urbanizing world. The hottest battles have moved down from the U.S. Forest Service-managed mountaintops, some of which have gained protection as Congressionally-designated "wilderness," to the deserts and canyons overseen by the Bureau of Land Management (BLM). BLM lands are biologically and culturally rich, but they have traditionally been ignored by conservationists in favor of the West's spectacular high altitude "rock and ice" country.

Not any more. *Give and Take* focuses on these BLM lands and the remarkable events that led to the creation of 20 national monuments and protected areas on BLM lands between 1996 and 2000. It was a period of time during which the BLM grew out of its image as an agency that cared more about cows and oil wells than scenery and wildlife. It was also a time of rapid change in the American West itself, as floods of new people transformed cities and towns seemingly overnight.

This book starts with Bill Clinton's dramatic decision to protect the 1.7 million-acre Grand Staircase-Escalante National Monument in southern Utah and takes us all the way to the present, in which the Bush administration has tried to return the BLM to its old energy-development habits.

The news stories, features, and essays we include here were all published in *High Country News* or the Writers on the Range editorial syndication service between 1996 and 2003. Pulled together, they are a parable for our times, revealing all of the issues and emotions that characterize this region's environmental struggles. The people of the West have always had an uneasy relationship with the federal government, which oversees more than half of the land base. We depend on the federal government for basic resources, such as water, and the right to graze livestock, cut logs, dig for minerals, or recreate on the public domain. And this dependency breeds discontent, because sometimes the federal government gives, and sometimes it takes.

In *Give and Take*, this troubled relationship appears over and over again, as the Clinton administration uses both the carrot and the stick to create a public lands legacy in the West.

What you will not find in the book are the tumultuous events that led the administration to its monumental strategy. In 1992, environmentalists felt as if they had struck gold when the newly elected Clinton administration immediately went after two sacred cows in the West: public lands grazing and mining. But the initial optimism that environmentally destructive mining and grazing would soon be reigned in wilted quickly as Clinton's point man, Secretary of Interior Bruce Babbitt, traveled around the West stumping for reform. Everywhere Babbitt went, he was greeted by waves of angry ranchers, miners, loggers, county commissioners, state officials, and members of Congress. The strength of the opposition flustered the administration, and after taking a few lumps, it quickly backed off on grazing reform. Reform of the archaic 1872 Mining Law died soon thereafter in the halls of Congress.

Then in 1994, at the mid-term elections, Republicans took full charge of Congress, and the once-golden prospects for protecting public lands darkened further. Clinton even OK'd the Salvage Logging rider, which gave timber companies one more whack at the forests in the Pacific Northwest.

As the 1996 Presidential election drew near, Clinton's team needed an environmental victory. That's when it dusted off a law that gave it unilateral authority to protect public lands. The Antiquities Act of 1906 had been used by Presidents since the days of Teddy Roosevelt to protect lands with significant natural, historical, and cultural resources as national monuments, including the Grand Canyon, Grand Tetons and Zion. And the beauty of it was, it didn't involve Congress at all.

And so in the fall of 1996, on the eve of the election, Bill Clinton stood on the edge of the Grand Canyon and declared the creation of the Grand Staircase-Escalante National Monument in southern Utah, the first of 20 new protected areas he would sign into law before leaving office in 2000.

This is where our play begins.

ACT I

THE CURTAIN RISES

President Clinton at Grand Canyon, September 18, 1996,
proclaims new national monument

INTERIOR VIEW I

Former High Country News *publisher Ed Marston interviewed Interior Secretary Bruce Babbitt on February 12, 2001, President Clinton's and Babbitt's last day in office.*

BABBITT: Ed, it's a pleasure to talk to you. It's my last day in office and it's a great way to spend it.

MARSTON: Is it hectic for you today?

BABBITT: Well, we'd had a lot of things that had been in the pipeline for five, six or seven months, and yeah, actually, we've got a lot to do. I signed documents creating a million acres of new wildlife refuges just last night.

MARSTON: Looking back on what is now almost a full eight years, was there a high point?

BABBITT: Sure. I think the high point has been the last 12 months. All the hard work of those early years—the really tough slogging around, working on Habitat Conservation Plans, working to lay the groundwork for these (new national) monuments—all came together.

A BOLD STROKE: CLINTON TAKES A 1.7 MILLION-ACRE STAND IN UTAH

by Paul Larmer

∽❧

"GOD'S HANDIWORK IS EVERYWHERE in the natural beauty of the Escalante Canyons and in the Kaiparowits Plateau, in the rock formations that show layer by layer the billions of years of geology, in the fossil record of dinosaurs and other prehistoric life, in the remains of ancient civilizations like the Anasazi Indians.

"In protecting it, we live up to our obligation to preserve our natural heritage. We are saying simply, 'Our parents and grandparents saved the Grand Canyon for us; today, we will save the grand Escalante Canyons and the Kaiparowits Plateau of Utah for our children.'"[1]

Though the day starts cool and gray, by noon the sun breaks through the clouds, casting golden rays on some 2,000 people gathered on the south rim of Arizona's Grand Canyon. Environmentalists, Native Americans, government bureaucrats, politicians, scholars, and even a few movie stars mingle in the warm September light, excitedly awaiting a pronouncement.

As the ceremony begins, a few Hopi elders rise and deliver a blessing: "This is a time of healing," they say. "The healing must begin."

---

[1] President Bill Clinton, Sept. 18, 1996

Then, with a stroke of his pen, President Clinton signs a document establishing 1.7 million acres in southern Utah as the Grand Staircase-Escalante National Monument. Thanks to the little-known Antiquities Act of 1906, which grants the president executive powers to designate new monuments, the declaration is final. No Congress, no mind-numbing or raucous public hearings, no mess: "Here Utah, have a monument."

The crowd roars its approval, but three men wearing black ribbons on their lapels stand quietly in the back. Perhaps the only time they smile during the ceremony is when the chopping of a helicopter interrupts Utah writer and wilderness advocate Terry Tempest Williams at the precise moment she asks the assembly to "listen to the silence." These three men from Kane County, the home of the new monument, are virtually the only Utah officials present, and they are mad as hell.

> NO CONGRESS, NO MIND-NUMBING OR RAUCOUS PUBLIC HEARINGS, NO MESS: 'HERE UTAH, HAVE A MONUMENT.'

After all, the battle over wilderness has raged for more than a decade here. County commissioners sent bulldozers into proposed wilderness areas one Fourth of July, wilderness supporters have been hung in effigy, and environmentalists have decided that compromise and consensus are dirty words. It remains to be seen whether the designated monument will heal Utah's environmental war, or prolong it.

Following the announcement at the Grand Canyon, solemn and angry locals in Kanab, Utah, 70 miles to the north, file into the high school gym for their own ceremony. To protest their loss of rights, they wear black arm bands and bear signs reading, "Shame on you Clinton" and "Why Clinton, Why? You're our President." And while environmentalists in Washington, D.C., release festively colored balloons on tethers, schoolchildren in Kanab free 50 black balloons to symbolically warn other states that the president could unilaterally lock away their lands, too.

For six years, Kanab, population 3,000, has eagerly awaited coal development by Andalex, a Dutch-owned company that would tap into a motherlode of coal—62 billion tons according to a recent federal analysis—under the remote, grassy Kaiparowits Plateau. The 50-year project was to provide locals with hundreds of decent-paying jobs and billions of dollars in state and local taxes. Now, with one simple proclamation, Clinton had derailed the plan.

Utah's mostly Republican congressional delegation, which fought hard to keep the Kaiparowits open to mining, blasted Clinton for steamrolling Westerners. "This is the mother of all land grabs," said Sen. Orrin Hatch, R-Utah. "An outrageous, arrogant approach to public policy," echoed fellow Utah Republican Sen. Bob Bennett.

Rep. James Hansen, R-Utah, vowed to cripple the monument by stripping it of funds, while state and county officials began crafting a legal challenge to the designation. The outrage wasn't confined to Utah. Sen. Larry Craig, R-Idaho, immediately introduced a bill to prevent the president from making a similar designation in his state without full public participation and congressional approval.

The monument will not be managed by the National Park

Service, but by the Bureau of Land Management (BLM), which already administers the area and has long-standing relationships with local communities. Grazing, hunting, and fishing will still be allowed.

This helps some, but not a lot: "I'd like to see local people involved," said Kane County Commissioner Joe Judd. "I'd like to see taxes for school trust lands (in the monument), and I'd like to see 900 well-paying jobs. But I come across as un-American because the president says this land should be a national monument. Well, the reason this land is so beautiful is because we've been taking care of it for the last 150 years."

Before Clinton's announcement, but after rumors had been leaked to the national press, Judd flew back to Washington, D.C., to confront White House officials. "They said they knew nothing about it," he said. "Then the next day we find out it's a done deal and that it's been in the works for four months."

Even some environmentalists felt miffed by the administration's secretiveness. "All kinds of people I work with are angry about the process that didn't happen," said Bill Hedden, a Grand County council member who also works for Grand Canyon Trust, the environmental group that helped host the ceremony.

And while newspapers on either coast ran glowing editorials about the plan, most Utah papers—even the generally pro-environment *Salt Lake Tribune*—took positions decrying the lack of public participation, if not the plan itself.

FROM DEFENSE TO OFFENSE

Behind the anger, some Utahns were searching their souls. How had control over public land management been so easily wrested from their hands? And would the new monument divide or unite the state in its future struggles over wilderness designation?

Less than a year before, the state's political leaders seemed on the verge of resolving the struggle over Utah's unprotected wild lands once and for all. They passed legislation based on county recommendations that would have designated as wilderness approximately 1.8 million acres of land controlled by the Bureau of Land Management. The rest would have been thrown open to development, including large portions of the Kaiparowits Plateau.

Environmentalists complained bitterly about the delegation's bill—they were pushing for 5.7 million acres of BLM wilderness —and the process, which they said gave too much influence to rural counties and ignored pro-environmental sentiments in Utah's densely-populated Wasatch Front.

Led by the Southern Utah Wilderness Alliance, environmentalists nationalized the debate, calling on people across the country to stand up for Utah's magnificent wild lands, to pressure their members of Congress to defeat the Utah delegation's wilderness bill. It worked. In December 1995, opposition within the House of Representatives forced Rep. Hansen to pull his bill before a vote.

The defeat created a political vacuum, and into it stepped the Clinton administration. One anonymous White House official says administration staffers had been on the lookout for environmental victories they could achieve without congressional support. They'd considered making Alaska's Arctic National Wildlife Refuge a national monument, but decided that the president could use his veto powers to stop destructive oil drilling in the refuge, so they targeted Utah instead. A team from the Department of the Interior, including Interior Solicitor John Leshy, and some outsiders, was asked to work out the details. Administration officials involved realized the designation was a stroke of political genius. It would resonate well with a public irritated at Republican efforts to roll back environmental laws and regulations; it would shore up the president's green credentials; and it wouldn't affect Clinton's prospects in Utah, where he had finished third behind Ross Perot in 1992. Some say Clinton also got swept away by enthusiasm after announcing a month earlier that the administration would halt a gold mine near Yellowstone National Park. "It's fun to be president; let's do some more of this," he reportedly told a nearby staffer at the park ceremony.

But it seems that even the administration was caught a little off-guard. Officials were still crafting the monument proposal when reporter Frank Clifford of the *Los Angeles Times* broke news of it. Then it appeared in the *Washington Post*, and the White House decided it could wait no longer.

ADMINISTRATION OFFICIALS INVOLVED REALIZED THE DESIGNATION WAS A STROKE OF POLITICAL GENIUS.

Already, officials were inundated with pleas from both sides. Utah's delegation begged the president's staff to back off and let Utahns decide the fate of the wildest country left in the lower 48 states. They told Clinton that Utah's schoolchildren would suffer if Andalex couldn't develop and pay fees on 200,000 acres of school trust lands scattered throughout the proposed monument. Finally, they resorted to name-calling in the media: They said the president was a midnight land-grabber seeking to burnish his image just weeks before the November election. Some even charged that environmentalists cozy with the administration had crafted the proposal.

Utah environmentalists denied the allegation and said the Utah congressional delegation itself had set the stage for Clinton's decision.

"The stars were aligned," said an exultant Ken Rait of the Southern Utah Wilderness Alliance. "The backdrop was created by the arrogance of the Utah delegation which snubbed much of its constituency. It pushed a wilderness bill that tried to bring down the spirit and intent of the wilderness act, (and that) put Utah public lands on the national map."

Added the Grand Canyon Trust's Hedden: "The creation of the monument was a reaction to the fact that we are so polarized in this state that we can't communicate at all with each other. We have failed to come up with a solution on our own, so basically we took ourselves out of the debate."

WHAT HAPPENS NOW?

Will Utahns hold a permanent grudge or will they sit down together to craft an agreeable management plan for the monument?

So far, cooperation seems unlikely. Kane County Commissioner Judd says his county will now back away from an expected agreement with state and federal agencies to reintroduce California condors to the area. "We're not going to sign it now," said Judd. "If one of those condors sits its butt in the monument, why, then, we've got an endangered species problem."

"We're going to be a whole lot less cooperative with the federal government," echoes Kane County's attorney Colin Winchester. "I know it's playground stuff—you know, my daddy's bigger than yours—but that's the way we feel now."

Others believe that the president's move will ultimately be seen as a watershed leading to more peaceful resolutions of public land issues. Writer Terry Tempest Williams says she believes many Utahns support the monument. "To hear what's going on in the papers, you'd think Utah is in a wake," she said. "But my family is Republican and they're absolutely thrilled. This is one important step toward a growing conservation ethic that we are seeing in Utah. I think things will calm down and the hard work will begin."

> THE CREATION OF THE MONUMENT WAS A REACTION TO THE FACT THAT WE ARE SO POLARIZED IN THIS STATE THAT WE CAN'T COMMUNICATE AT ALL WITH EACH OTHER.

Pollsters at the *Salt Lake Tribune* are waiting for the anger to subside before trying to find out what Utahns really think. The *Deseret News*, however, released an early poll showing 49 percent opposed to the monument and 29 percent for it; 61 percent said the process used to create it was unfair.

Beyond the immediate question of the monument lurks the larger question of how much additional public land in Utah should be designated wilderness. Some environmentalists fear the monument will be the extent of it for a long, long time.

Others say it strengthens their hand. Says Tempest Williams, "I view (the monument) as a down payment."

One precedent for such a view is Alaska. Following President Jimmy Carter's designation of some 56 million acres of national monuments there in 1978, Alaska's congressional delegation began holding serious talks with industry leaders and environmentalists about which lands warranted protection and which could be exploited for resources. The result: the 1980 Alaska Lands Act, the largest and perhaps most remarkable piece of public-lands legislation in the last century.

Optimists might also take heart from a marquee outside a roadside business in Kanab. Clinton is clearly a villain, but the monument could be something locals warm to. "Shame on you Clinton," read the sign. Then below: "Buses welcome."

September 30, 1996

CLINTON LEARNS THE ART OF AUDACITY

by *Charles Wilkinson*

THE GRANDEST, MOST ELECTRIFYING moments in American conservation history have always been reserved for the setting aside of large blocks of pristine land for protection.

Yellowstone. Yosemite. Glacier. Olympic. Teton. Rocky Mountain. The Grand Canyon.

Our presidents have played a central role in protecting large land areas. During the 19th century, the pressures on wild land had not yet built up and the calls for protection were few. Then the 20th century dawned and gave us Theodore Roosevelt, the most courageous, the most audacious, the most outrageous—and therefore the greatest—conservation president.

Roosevelt ignited the long, proud tradition of presidential activism for the land.

Take, for example, 1903 and five-acre Pelican Island off the coast of Florida. The island may have been small, but the history T.R. wrote was large and spirited. Roosevelt wanted to make Pelican Island, all federal land, what he called a national wildlife refuge. He inquired of the Justice Department as to his power to do this.

A few days later, a government lawyer, sallow, squinty-eyed, pursed-lipped—a classic lawyer—came to the White House. He solemnly intoned, "I cannot find a law that will allow you to do this, Mr. President."

"But," replied T.R., now rising to his full height, "is there a law that will prevent it?" The lawyer, now frowning, replied that no, there was not. T.R. responded, "Very well, I so declare it."

The Antiquities Act of 1906 has been the single most important vehicle for presidential conservation action. It gives broad power to the president, and the great conservation presidents, T.R., F.D.R., and Carter, have used it extensively and courageously to designate national monuments to protect, as the Act says, "objects of historic or scientific interest." Carter's designation of 56 million acres as monuments in Alaska has been called the greatest single action in conservation history.

The objection to Carter's action was that the Antiquities Act limits monuments to the "smallest area compatible with the proper care and management of the objects to be protected."

At first blush, Carter might seem to have been reaching a bit. After all, the Antiquities Act was proposed by the archaeologist Edgar Lee Hewett, who seemed to have had in mind specific digs—and a maximum of 640 acres. Carter's 17 monuments averaged more than 3 million acres.

By the time Carter acted for Alaska, a long-shadowed precedent had already been set. In 1908 T.R. set aside, as the "smallest area compatible," quite a large canyon in northern Arizona and the Supreme Court had upheld it. Today, the courts allow presidents broad leeway with the Antiquities Act.

This Colorado Plateau has the greatest concentration of

national parks and monuments in the world. Some of the following places are now parks but they all began as national monuments. We owe their existence to the Antiquities Act, brought to vivid life by presidential courage and foresight.

Listen to the beauty and wonder and magic in these words: Canyon de Chelly. Wupatki. Petrified Forest. Cedar Breaks. Navajo. Colorado. Zion. Arches. Natural Bridges. Rainbow Bridge. Hovenweep. Capitol Reef. Bryce Canyon. Chaco Canyon. The Grand Canyon.

Now we have received the lasting gift of another national monument. At 1.7 million acres, half again the size of Grand Canyon National Park, it is one of the largest national monuments ever created in the lower 48 states. It features twisty, redrock canyons and long, high plateaus; and arches and natural bridges; and fine sites where the Old People, the Anasazi, lived and loved. It encompasses part of the Grand Staircase.

> [THE KAIPAROWITS PLATEAU IS] THE LAST PLACE TO BE MAPPED, THE FARTHEST-AWAY PLACE, LITERALLY THE MOST REMOTE PLACE IN THE CONTINENTAL UNITED STATES.

At its center is a high, remote, bell-shaped plateau called Kaiparowits, the last place to be mapped, the farthest-away place, literally the most remote place in the continental United States. It would seem an impossible candidate for national monument status, holding, as it does, a high-BTU, low-sulphur coal deposit that is as good as any on Earth.

How could this country have the will to leave such a place be, to stay our hand, to pass on the coal? But, through presidential courage and wisdom and spirit, we can now say these words: Grand Staircase-Escalante National Monument.

We are so blessed to be in this place, this exact place at this moment. For history's eagles fly high today, sailing and rolling and turning in the currents above us, lending their resolve and strength and approval to the brave and true act.

And we know they also ride the thermals rising up off the Circle Cliffs, the Straight Cliffs, the Cockscomb, and the Grand Staircase. Looking out, taking the long view, the eagles of history see the land, always the land, a rough and rocky but magnificent and sacred land, finally, at last, safe today.

September 30, 1996

THE MOTHER OF
ALL LAND GRABS

by Paul Larmer

❧

SEN. ORRIN HATCH, R-UTAH:

"In all my 20 years in the U.S. Senate, I have never seen a clearer example of the arrogance of federal power. Indeed, this is the mother of all land grabs. And, the declaration by President Clinton is being made without so much as a by-your-leave to the people of Utah.

"There has been no consultation; no hearings; no town meetings; no TV or radio discussion shows; no input from federal land managers 'on the ground'; no maps, no boundaries; no nothing. In fact, we first had to learn about this matter from the *Washington Post* just a week ago.

"It is utterly apparent that the public processes mandated by our existing environmental laws, such as the National Environmental Policy Act, have not been followed. These processes exist precisely to prevent this kind of federal usurpation of state and local prerogatives without public knowledge or debate. And, what should be clear to everyone in a state with public land is that if the president can exercise such power with regard to Utah, then he can exercise it where you live as well.

"Moreover, the declaration has nothing to do with preserving land in southern Utah—which is a goal we all share—and everything to do with scoring political points with a powerful interest group just 48 days before a national election. Isn't it interesting that adherence to an open, public process, where policy decisions are made in the light of day, has always been advocated by environmental groups? But now, when it serves their own purposes, these groups remain silent and refrain from crying foul to a deal crafted behind closed doors.

"The president may have some statutory authority to take this action, but he certainly does not have the moral authority."

September 30, 1996

A HARSH AND PRICELESS GIFT TO THE WORLD

by Diane Sylvain

⋆

"THERE WAS A HARDNESS OF STONE," Theodore Roethke starts a poem, "an uncertain glory…Between cliffs of light/We strayed like children."

The Harsh Country, the poem is called. I'm miles away from what I think of as the harsh country, the cliffs of light, the country of bright stone. It has a new name now, to be layered on top of its other names, Anglo and Spanish and Indian, spoken and silent. It's the Grand Staircase-Escalante National Monument.

I have maps in front of me. I know some of the names the new monument gathers: Kaiparowits, No Man's Mesa, Burning Hills, Paria. I know of the ravens and the rattlesnakes there, and the potsherds and the canyons and the dark nights full of stars. I'm a painter, and the landscape is a palette for me: Pink Cliffs, White Cliffs, Vermilion Cliffs.

I love maps and I draw maps, so I look at these maps and dream. In my backpacking days, I nibbled around the edges of the Escalante, with a short hike here and there. I planned long trips that never got made; you know how it goes. Now an injury makes it hard for me to hike, but that doesn't matter, really. I didn't need to go there to love it. And now the maps have been saved for me.

Not everyone is as happy as I am about the monument. Some environmentalists are disappointed because we wanted more, and we wanted it as wilderness. Some are so cynical about President Clinton's motives and timing that they can't get the bad taste out of their mouths. That doesn't bother me in the least. Even Lincoln signed the Emancipation Proclamation with politics in mind. The main thing is, he signed it.

THE FACT IS, THE ESCALANTE IS, AND ALWAYS HAS BEEN, AS MUCH MINE AND YOURS AS UTAH'S.

I feel sorry for those Utah locals who feel blind-sided and run over by a train, but not as sorry as they want me to feel. I have small-town ancestors myself, in places like Georgia, who have been blind-sided in the past, by things like the freeing of the slaves. Times change everywhere. It is possible to adapt.

The fact is, the Escalante is, and always has been, as much yours and mine as Utah's. Calling it a national monument may be the only way to make that clear.

As for the Utah delegation: I can't help but smile to think of their anti-wilderness bluster brought to a spluttering, foam-mouthed stop by this sweet checkmate move. It makes me want to burst into song: "Locking up the Kaiparowits/Causes the Utah congressmen fits!"

Of course they'll accuse us of "locking up" their public lands. What an interesting choice of words that is: locking up the land. You lock something up so it can't escape. But the harsh country, the bright country, could never be kept locked up. It's escaping now, all the time, coming through all barriers, sending out tendrils of barberry perfume, leaking sandstone grit and raven shadows. That's why we needed to save it. That's why we honor its place on our maps.

We didn't need the coal buried there. The Escalante is a furnace already, giving heat and light and burning power. People who will never see it in person, people in Florida and Japan and England and Ohio, will look at their maps, at that space saved for mystery, and warm their hands over it in their dreaming. This is what I'm doing now.

I dream over the map of southern Utah the way I wonder over the stars at night. Each is a chart to a country I may not visit; each guides me, powers me, lights me nonetheless.

The Harsh Country.

Orion. Jupiter. The Andromeda galaxy.

Kaiparowits. Paria. The Grand Staircase-Escalante.

September 30, 1996

ACT II

THE FALLOUT

Grosverner Arch, South of Tropic, Utah

INTERIOR VIEW II

by Ed Marston

$\sim$

MARSTON: Just before he was re-elected in fall 1996, President Clinton declared his first national monument, Grand Staircase-Escalante. Was that important?

BABBITT: The important thing about the Grand Staircase-Escalante National Monument was not only the declaration of the land-scape…but the decision to make it a monument managed by the Bureau of Land Management. In 100 years of use of the (Antiquities) Act, presidents have reflexively used it to declare national monuments and then transfer them over to the National Park Service.

When this one came along, I said to the president, 'We ought to do this differently. Because, by continually robbing the BLM of its crown jewels, we're reinforcing this kind of defeatist image that the BLM is nothing but livestock and mining.'…Of the twenty-some odd monuments that have been declared by the president since then, I think 19 of them have remained in the BLM.

MARSTON: Why is it that you have a soft spot for the BLM, which is on everyone's list of bad agencies?

BABBITT: The environmentalists have demonized the BLM over the years as a sort of doormat for the mining and grazing industry. If you spend all of your time demonizing an agency, ultimately your predictions will come true.

MARSTON: But you must have seen something about the BLM the environmentalists didn't see.

BABBITT: Well, sure, I grew up with the BLM on all sides of where we ranched, where I went to school in Arizona. And what I knew then, and know now, is that the BLM is an agency full of a lot of different kinds of people, and many of them would be happy to perform to higher standards. What they need is some leadership and an opportunity and some incentive.

MARSTON: Why did the administration create Grand Staircase-Escalante in that 'stealth' way, without even consulting with Utah officials?

BABBITT: Well, I think the main reason is, it was a campaign year, and the rules, you know, tend to get a little unsettled when you are in a national campaign. I understand that there is still some residue from that.

February 12, 2001

UTAH COUNTIES BULLDOZE THE BLM, PARK SERVICE

by Larry Warren

❧

A FLURRY OF BULLDOZING in three southern Utah counties has led to one arrest, federal lawsuits, and miles of newly improved roadways through wilderness study areas and the new Grand Staircase-Escalante National Monument.

The bulldozing, ordered by county commissioners in San Juan, Garfield, and Kane counties, is the most serious challenge yet to federal land managers trying to maintain wilderness qualities in areas they manage. It is also a sign of increasing anger and frustration by county commissioners in southern Utah.

"They want to blade these roads so they can assure there will never be wilderness," said angry activist Ken Sleight of the recent confrontations. "It's tragic, but that's the way it is. They're ticked off about wilderness and the president's establishment of Grand Staircase-Escalante National Monument."

On October 18, the federal government filed lawsuits in U.S. District Court in Salt Lake City, asking for trespass damages and injunctions against the three counties. U.S. Attorney Scott Matheson Jr. is seeking a permanent court order to halt further road grading in disputed areas and monetary damages to rehabilitate the roads already bladed. A handful of people, including Sleight, tried to stop the road-building by San Juan County September 30 by standing in front of a county road-grader on Hart's Point near Canyonlands National Park.

One protester, 33-year-old Dan Kent of Moab, Utah, was charged with disorderly conduct, resisting arrest and "failure to disperse."

His arrest came after the Bureau of Land Management's area resource manager, Kent Walter, tried to stop the county with a cease-and-desist order. The county ignored the order by blading 10.7 miles of road across BLM land being considered for wilderness designation.

At issue is the county's assertion that it has legal rights of way across federal lands anywhere a vehicle has been driven and left a track. Utah counties claim such rights of way under a Civil War-era statute called RS 2477, which states, "The right of way for the construction of highways over public lands, not reserved for public uses, is hereby granted."

For years, Utah counties have feuded with the BLM over the interpretation of the statute, which Congress repealed 20 years ago. Counties argue that any route across public land is a legal right of way that the county can claim as a road and maintain.

The BLM does not consider faint, revegetated jeep tracks as roads, and will not rule out such tracked areas for wilderness study. The Hart's Point land is not an official BLM Wilderness Study Area, but the Utah Wilderness Coalition wants it included as part of its 5.7 million-acre wilderness proposal.

San Juan County officials admit the road grader was intentionally sent out to make a point and force a lawsuit.

"Until a judge tells us they're not our roads, we're going to continue," County Commissioner Bill Redd said. "Just because someone doesn't like it doesn't mean he can tell me to quit."

County commissioners said after roads were bladed on Hart's Point, they might move on to Cedar Mesa, the archaeologically rich land which includes Grand Gulch.

"If they so much as put a blade down and move one inch (on Cedar Mesa), we'll file an ARPA (Archaeological Resource Protection Act) violation against them," the BLM's Walter warned while inspecting the road-grading on Hart's Point.

The federal lawsuits allege, in addition to San Juan's grading, that Garfield County in early October graded short sections of road on the Right Hand Collet Canyon Trail and in the Devil's Garden Wilderness Study Area. They say the county graded longer six-mile sections in both Cedar Wash and the Wolverine Loop. All four bulldozed roads are within the boundaries of Grand Staircase-Escalante National Monument.

> UNTIL A JUDGE TELLS US THEY'RE NOT OUR ROADS, WE'RE GOING TO CONTINUE. JUST BECAUSE SOMEONE DOESN'T LIKE IT DOESN'T MEAN HE CAN TELL ME TO QUIT.

Another lawsuit accuses Kane County of blading approximately 15 miles of roads within three wilderness study areas: Moquith Mountain, Burning Hills, and Paria-Hackberry.

And Garfield County is being sued by the National Park Service for bulldozing inside Capitol Reef National Park along the Burr Trail. That February 13 bulldozing by Garfield County crews over the objections of the Park Service resulted in a widening of the road from its original 18 feet width to as much as 32 feet wide. The Park Service says the county excavated away hillsides that had framed the east entrance to the park. Federal attorneys in the Burr Trail case were quoted in court documents as saying Garfield County has a habit of "bulldozing first and apologizing later."

October 28, 1996

THIS MONUMENT WAS JUST PLAIN STUPID

by Paul Larmer

❧

"THIS MONUMENT WAS JUST PLAIN STUPID."

Roger Holland, 52, is a Kanab town councilman, a part-time rancher and a mining consultant. He has done geological surveys on the Kaiparowits Plateau within the Grand Staircase-Escalante National Monument.

Roger Holland: "This monument was just plain stupid; the president did it to keep people from voting for Ralph Nader.

"We can have a coal mine and wilderness. I've been going out to the (Andalex) mine site regularly since 1988, and I've never seen a backpacker on the Kaiparowits. Andalex would have provided 2.5 million tons a year off of 40 acres you couldn't see unless you were actually up there. But the environmentalists want to control all that country.

"The Kaiparowits coal is the best we have left. There's nowhere else Clinton can send Andalex to get a similar resource. It's like someone taking your Rolls Royce and saying, 'I'm going to give you the pick of the Ford lot.'"

"America will become a Third World nation if we don't pull our head out. Corporate America is getting sent abroad because it's too hard to do business here. I'm going to be one mad José when my kids get killed at war in the Middle East because we haven't developed the resources here."

April 14, 1997

BEAUTY AND THE BEAST:
The President's New Monument Forces
Southern Utah to Face Its Tourism Future

by Paul Larmer

⚜

OUTSIDE THE KANE COUNTY administration building, a warm autumn sun sets the red cliffs ablaze. Inside, seated in front of an American flag, Kane County's own firebrand, Joe Judd, 67, tells how he came to this small town in southernmost Utah.

"I retired 17 years ago as parks manager for the city of L.A.," he says. "I was responsible for 200 parks, 14 golf courses, and a staff of 2,200 that was 80 percent black."

Judd says the job was rewarding, but ate him alive. "You don't get to be a nice guy when you have your life threatened," he says, shaking his head. "So when I was 50, I said, 'I don't need this.'" He moved to Kanab.

Instead of hobby ranching, Judd became active in the Mormon Church, serving as a bishop and helping overhaul a soup kitchen for the needy. He also served on the board of the local power company. Then, two years ago, he won a seat on the Kane County Commission.

"Now I'm working on zoning ordinances and septic regulations," he says. "I'm trying to pull people here into the 20th century."

This Joe Judd seems far different from the one I talked to two months ago, the day after President Bill Clinton created the 1.7 million-acre Grand Staircase-Escalante National Monument. The monument, more than half of which lies in Kane County, killed a proposed coalmine on the Kaiparowits Plateau that supporters say would have brought millions of dollars into Kanab and other towns in the area.

On the phone, Judd cursed the Clinton administration for running roughshod over local people and for destroying the last hope for good wages in his county, which is 95 percent public land and home to just 10,000 people. Soon after, Judd and his fellow commissioners sent county bulldozers into the new monument, some to areas environmentalists want protected as roadless wilderness.

Judd still curses the president and is unapologetic about the "freshened up" roads. But he quickly accepted $100,000 from the Clinton administration to do planning in conjunction with the new monument, and then asked for and received $100,000 that neighboring Garfield County had rejected as "blood money." His county then signed an "assistance agreement" with the Bureau of Land Management that spells out how the two will cooperate during the planning process for the monument.

"It was arrogant as hell for the president to use the law to his advantage as he did," the commissioner says. "But we're not going to sit around with our heads in our hands."

Before visiting southern Utah, I couldn't have guessed that Kane County might embrace the new monument. But Judd and others like him recognize that the monument solidifies two facts of life: Southern Utah's mining, logging and ranching are in decline; and the region is already a public-lands playground for the world.

Even the angry leaders in Garfield County, which is home to the monument's northern half, recognize that the game has evolved from fighting off outsiders to adapting to a tourism boom that could turn their quiet towns into theme parks.

As I drove for hours around the edges of this immense monument and visited its widely scattered communities, I wondered how the land and the people would change over the coming years. Would the anger and resentment fade? Would the Bureau of Land Management be able to run a monument that will attract millions of visitors each year? And would the towns end up looking and feeling like every other strip-developed community near a national treasure?

IT WAS ARROGANT AS HELL FOR THE PRESIDENT TO USE THE LAW TO HIS ADVANTAGE AS HE DID.

KANE COUNTY: PROSPERITY'S THIN VENEER

Kanab, population 4,500, boasts a golf course on the edge of town that bustles on a weekday in mid-November, and newish hotels, gift stores, and restaurants line the clean, wide streets. It seems downright prosperous for a town that has just seen its hopes for a major industrial project—the Andalex coal mine—dashed.

A mild climate and proximity to some of the southwest's finest scenery have made tourism the town's main economic force for years. Bryce Canyon, Zion, Grand Canyon, and Capitol Reef national parks are all closer than a day's drive, as is Lake Powell. The Grand Staircase-Escalante National Monument is just the latest and nearest attraction.

But not long ago, tourism was balanced by a substantial natural-resource-based economy. The scales tipped during the early 1990s, when Kanab lost more than 500 timber and uranium mining jobs. Families that had a primary breadwinner earning $20 to $30 an hour suddenly had to move or change occupations. Those who wanted to stay had to send Dad to work as a trucker or laborer in a distant city and add Mom, grandma, and the kids to the work force, most often cleaning hotel rooms and flipping hamburgers for tourists at $5 an hour.

In 1990, 1.5 people per Kane County household were in the work force and the average income was $25,000, according to a recent economic report prepared for the county. Today, 2.6 people per household work and the average income has eroded to $18,000.

"When the high-paying jobs dried up, more people had to work just to meet the bills," says Gil Miller, a Logan, Utah-based economist who drafted Kane County's latest economic development plan. "The only jobs available were in the tourism industry."

Kanab councilman Roger Holland says seven families in his Mormon Church ward lost their jobs with the closure of the Kaibab mill. "Some have gone on unemployment, then welfare," Holland says. "None of these families have come back to the point economically that they were before."

Tourism has continued to grow, but workers not only earn low wages, they frequently get laid off during the cold winter months. Roger Carter, manager of the Red Hills Best Western in Kanab, says he pares his summer staff of 35 to a baker's dozen during November, December, and January.

"We love our tourists, especially now that they're all we have," says Carter, who moved his family to Kanab seven years ago from Flagstaff, Arizona. "But it's a boom-and-bust economy, too."

To this hard-hit community, the Andalex coal mine project looked like a savior. No wonder everyone was hopping mad when the president took that hope away.

PRACTICAL TO THE CORE

Later that evening, I meet with three men who have moved past anger to focus on Kane County's future. They lead a community organization called CORE—Coalition of Resources and Economies.

On my left is hotel manager, Roger Carter, who serves as CORE's president; on my right, Richard Negus, a 67-year-old London-born transplant who has been an animal-rights activist, journalist, and cat-show announcer at New York's Madison Square Garden. Dead ahead of me is the imposing figure of Jim Matson, the former manager of Kaibab Industries' logging mill in Fredonia, Arizona, nine miles south of Kanab. The mill closed two years ago, a victim of changing economic conditions and, according to Matson, appeals of federal timber sales on the Kaibab National Forest north of the Grand Canyon brought by environmentalists.

"Do you have any environmentalists in your group?" I ask.

"All 12 of us," quips Matson.

A forester by training, Matson, 52, has been reborn as a

super-consultant on natural-resource conflicts and economic development. Kane County recently hired his firm to spend $200,000 in monument planning monies.

"We're a poor county, behind the times in land-use planning and economic development," he says. "The coal mine and the $1.5 million a year it would have provided—now that's gone and we have to quickly shift our priorities."

Matson says the monument catalyzed a countywide economic plan that he had been working on for months. The plan focuses on bringing small and medium-sized firms to the county—companies like Stamp 'Em Up, a business started in Las Vegas by two Kanab women who recently moved the operation back to their hometown. The company manufactures rubber impressions for a variety of crafts, and at 200 employees, it's Kane County's biggest employer.

> THE MONUMENT CATALYZED A COUNTYWIDE ECONOMIC PLAN THAT HE HAD BEEN WORKING ON FOR MONTHS.

But Matson knows Kanab is a rookie in the recruitment game. Last year, he says, the owners of a tent and outdoor-gear manufacturing company scouted Kanab as a possible location for their business. They left quickly when town officials couldn't promise that the company's sewer, water, power, and telecommunications needs would be met.

"We didn't even speak the same language," Matson recalls.

The new plan, which calls for zoning and upgrades in Kanab's infrastructure, should give the county the credibility it needs to start recruiting businesses from places like Southern California. It might be a tough sell.

Kanab's work force lacks the skills and expertise to attract the high-tech industries that are flocking to Utah's Wasatch Front, says economist Gil Miller. The nearest four-year college is several hours away, in Cedar City. And Kanab sits almost a hundred miles from an interstate and lacks commercial air service.

Kanab can't even attract the BLM. The agency recently decided to locate its temporary monument planning office in Cedar City, which is several hours away from the new monument and outside both Kane and Garfield counties. BLM monument supervisor Jerry Meredith says the agency didn't want to locate in any community near the monument for fear it would give the town an edge in the competition for permanent monument facilities. But there were logistical concerns as well, he admits.

Cedar City has an interstate, an airport, conference facilities, and Southern Utah University, Meredith says. And, it has real estate.

"We needed 6,000 square feet of space and 18 houses for employees right away," says Meredith. Even Kanab would have been marginal, he says.

To Matson, the BLM's decision was "a slap in the face. It said that they didn't want to live with us."

It also said Kane County would, for the next three years, lose out on 18 high-paying government jobs.

IF YOU DESIGNATE IT, WILL THEY COME?

Driving the 60 miles east from Kanab to Big Water, population 350, which lies within a few miles of Lake Powell, I am struck by

the immensity of the new monument. Its southern edge along
the highway is a series of rugged, sparsely vegetated cliffs that
extend as far as the eye can see.

The last protrusion is the Kaiparowits Plateau, which looms
like the prow of a giant ship behind the town of Big Water. It is
also the place where Andalex had planned to mine coal. Big
Water, with its dirt roads and boat-storage yards facing the highway, missed out on the mining boom, but its mayor, Gerry
Rankin, says she is eager to capitalize on the new monument.

It isn't a Grand Canyon or a Lake Powell, she says, "but it's
got a rough, difficult beauty, you might call it."

For Big Water to attract tourists, though, Rankin says it
needs the BLM to develop some roads into the monument so
that people can sightsee. The town also needs a sewer system, she
says. Without one, it has been unable to attract hotels or other
large commercial enterprises. The carloads of tourists now passing
Big Water on their way to Lake Powell have little reason to stop.

Joe Judd says he doubts the monument will give Big Water
much of a boost. The southern portion of the monument, he
says, is "like your big toe; there's nothing sexy about it. You won't
see anything that you can't find in two-thirds of the rest of the state."

There are few roads into the monument from the south,
Judd notes, and most are nearly impassable for all but skilled
four-wheel drivers. The people who come and want to see the
new monument will have to stay around the outskirts or risk
getting stuck or lost. Either way, they are a liability, in his view.

Judd recently jetted to Washington, D.C., with Garfield
County Commissioner Louise Liston to ask Congress for
$575,000 to help his county cope with everything from a

stretched police force to growing numbers of lost and injured hikers, and overflowing garbage bins. Liston asked for $900,000 and an extra $2 million for road maintenance and improvement in the monument.

By asking for so much money, Judd seems to contradict his prediction that the monument will generate little interest. But early readings indicate that tourists are chomping at the bit. The BLM offices in Kanab, Escalante, and Salt Lake City say they are swamped with thousands of requests for monument information and maps. A Web site put on the Internet by the town of Escalante's Chamber of Commerce received 2,000 hits during February alone.

THE BLM OFFICES IN KANAB, ESCALANTE, AND SALT LAKE CITY SAY THEY ARE SWAMPED WITH THOUSANDS OF REQUESTS FOR MONUMENT INFORMATION AND MAPS.

"We want all the tourism we can get," admits Matson, "but we don't want a Moab (Utah)-type situation," where hordes of visitors have failed to lift family income and strained public services to the breaking point.

Kane County's eager-but-cautious attitude toward tourism is based on experience. Even without the monument, towns like Kanab have begun to see the negative side of a minimum-wage economy and the outsiders it attracts. The newcomers may also have a tough time fitting in with the locals. The communities in Kane and Garfield counties share two characteristics: The citizens are predominately white and Mormon.

"The people that come down to fill these jobs have different values," says Tom Hatch, a sixth generation rancher who represents both Kane and Garfield counties in the state Legislature. "They work a season and then they go on welfare or unemployment. It's changed our schools and our kids. We have drugs and violence and some kids want to become gang members."

STEERING THE SHIP

Matson says the county will keep tourism's downside uppermost in its mind during the BLM's planning process. "We want to steer the ship rather than have someone steer it for us," he says.

Steering the ship means local control. The county wants monument visitor centers and staff offices located within communities such as Kanab and Escalante, not inside the monument. Environmentalists say they like that idea.

"There's no reason to put a Marriott in the middle of the Kaiparowits Plateau," says Scott Groene, an attorney with the Southern Utah Wilderness Alliance. "This is actually a place where we all agree."

Jerry Meredith says his agency will consider placing several visitor centers in the communities around the monument. "This monument is so spread out that it doesn't lend itself to having one central headquarters," says Meredith, who previously oversaw the monument area as the BLM's Cedar City district manager.

Kane County also wants to hire county employees to man new monument campgrounds and facilities. The idea of having local people filling these slots—instead of senior citizen volunteers or federal employees from afar—is novel.

"If we could get 150 jobs paying $8, $9 or $10 an hour with

benefits, that would be a whole lot more than we have now," says Richard Negus, CORE's public affairs director.

Meredith says the BLM will consider contracting out services to the counties, though it is too early to commit.

GARFIELD COUNTY: HOLDING TO THE PAST

Garfield County is Kane County's colder, rougher brother. It has some of the most scenic—and already well-visited—portions of the Grand Staircase-Escalante National Monument. (BLM officials say that more than 500,000 visited the monument area last year and this year the number is likely to boom.) But the county's cool and wet winter climate, compared to Kane County, also means a shorter tourism season. Its towns are smaller and scattered across a landscape that is more than 98 percent federally owned. All 4,000 county residents could fit into the town of Kanab.

It's snowing and raw as I drive through Panguitch, the county seat. And quiet. Only a handful of cars and trucks cluster around the open businesses—a grocery store and a gas station. Panguitch is the county's biggest town with a population of 1,400, but it looks like a carnival that has closed for the season. The museums, gift stores, and hotels are here, but no customers. The town lost a timber mill and nearly 100 jobs two years ago.

Twenty-five miles and maybe six cars later, a lone coyote scampers across the road as I turn in to Bryce Canyon National Park. Ruby's Inn stands guard just outside the park entrance; compared with Panguitch, it bustles. A busload of foreign tourists load up in front of the lodge, which is run by a local family; inside, several dozen tourists dine at the cafe and browse in a souvenir shop the size of a department store.

At 80 years old, Ruby's Inn is the economic heavy of Garfield County, employing nearly 500 people during the summer months. But the minimum-wage-plus-tips pay can't compare to wages provided by a coal mine or a timber mill.

The next lonely hour down the road runs right through portions of the Grand Staircase-Escalante National Monument. This northwestern side of the monument, with its hayfields surrounded by towering cliffs dotted with juniper and pine, seems a world away from the harsh desert I encountered near Big Water. And it is; it has taken me a whole day to travel around just the western half of the monument.

I finally reach Escalante, another Mormon-settled community where locals recently hung effigies of President Clinton and Interior Secretary Bruce Babbitt. There's a room at the Prospector's Inn, but only after I track down one of the owners washing her truck out back.

She asks me if I'm here to see the monument. "Well, take a look out the window," she says when I say yes. "Everything you see is the monument except for this little town."

THE WOMAN SAYS SHE DOUBTS THE MONUMENT WILL LEAD TO A BOOM IN ESCALANTE. BUT LATER...SHE SAYS HERS IS ONE OF THREE NEW HOTELS TO OPEN IN TOWN WITHIN THE LAST THREE YEARS.

The woman says she doubts the monument will lead to a boom in Escalante. But later, as she serves dinner at the restaurant behind the hotel, she says hers is one of three new hotels to open in town within the last three years. And someone recently bought one of the original old, brick, two-story, Mormon settlers' houses which abound in this town, intending to run a bed and breakfast.

Even here, in a settlement that looks much as it did a century ago, change is in the air.

LAS VEGAS MULCH

The next day, sitting in a cramped trailer office at the Utah Forest Products mill south of Escalante, manager Stephen Steed asks a question.

"How many people stayed at your hotel last night?"

Just me and one other, I say.

"Yeah, that was probably our state forester who's down from Salt Lake for the week," Steed says. "That means a traveling newspaperman and the state forestry guy took care of the tourist industry in Escalante last night. Try feeding that to your family."

Though Steed doesn't have much use for tourism, he's not mired in the past. The fourth-generation logger and his father ran the mill until it shut down here in 1993, and he learned from that experience. The new mill is financed by outside money and is a different animal. It is smaller, employing just 65, and it is more efficient, producing a variety of goods, including milled lumber and chips.

"There's no waste," says Steed. "We even ship the chips to Las Vegas. They mix them with fertilizer to make a landscaping mulch for all those subdivisions in the desert."

This value-added stuff is what Garfield County commissioners have started to look for. They recently hired a Salt Lake City-based consulting firm to help its ranchers market "riparian-free, monument beef," says consultant David Nimkin of Confluence Associates. Riparian-free, he says, means cows stay out of streams.

He also sees local logging companies producing finished products, such as furniture or floorboards. "There's a big market for softwood floors in the Salt Lake City area, but most of the wood comes from the southeastern United States," says Nimkin. "Why couldn't Utah fir and pine fill that need?"

The concept extends to the monument: Keep its 1.7 million acres rugged and relatively roadless, and instead of fast-food jobs you'd need guides and outfitters to lead dudes into the trackless interior, says the planning consultant. The guides could even educate visitors about the history and culture of the area.

> KEEP [GRAND STAIRCASE-ESCALANTE'S] 1.7 MILLION ACRES RUGGED AND RELATIVELY ROADLESS, AND INSTEAD OF FAST-FOOD JOBS YOU'D NEED GUIDES AND OUTFITTERS TO LEAD DUDES INTO THE TRACKLESS INTERIOR.

"These towns are never going to be gateway communities like Springdale (outside Zion National Park)," says Nimkin. "But they could market the monument as one of the last great, wild places, a place where you need a local guide to show you the deep dark secrets."

Utah Gov. Mike Leavitt is paying attention. He has promised to help Garfield and Kane counties plan for the changes that lie ahead. Leavitt's planning director, Brad Barber, says the state is setting up an economic development team that will help these communities find money for new business ventures and the roads and services they need.

"Where do we put the lodges? Do we have building codes? What do we want our town to look like? Do we want any old, ugly Motel 6 in town?" asks Barber. "These are the questions these communities need to face now."

THE PIONEER SPIRIT

Before leaving Escalante, I stop at the ranch of Garfield County commissioner Louise Liston. The scrappy and articulate Escalante native is known as a staunch defender of rural values. Yet she and her fifth-generation cattle-rancher husband, Robert, have adapted to a new West: They've given up on cattle and now raise ostriches.

The Listons trace their roots back to the Mormon pioneers who found a way across the tortuous terrain from Escalante southeast across the Colorado River. You can still travel The Hole-in-the-Rock route, which lies in the new monument, on a teeth-rattling dirt road.

"When you know of the sacrifices our pioneer ancestors made, you feel that it demands the same type of sacrifice from you," Liston says.

She says her son-in-law next door worked at the old sawmill which closed in 1993. He has yet to find a permanent job and that's been tough on Liston's daughter and their six children.

"My daughter started working at the Dairy Queen in Panguitch," she says. "Now she's driving 50 miles to work at

Ruby's Inn. They sacrifice to stay in the valley. You don't do that unless you love it."

More tourism in Escalante could mean that Liston's daughter could work closer to home, but that doesn't sit well, either. "It worries me that we'll turn into Moab and have resorts," says Liston. "We'd love to keep our farming community and our cowboy flavor. I believe that's what draws the tourists."

Louise Liston is a study in contradictions: As a county leader, she has refused to take monument planning money from a despised federal government, yet she recently asked Congress for $2.9 million to help the county cope with the monument. She would like the prosperity tourism could bring but despises tourism because she fears it will change her quiet community forever.

The contrast between Liston and Kane County Commissioner Joe Judd appears stark. Faced with rapid change, one holds to the past while the other reaches for the future. But as I head out Liston's door, she says, "You know, the monument is here, and we need to make the best of it."

EVERYONE SAYS THEY DON'T WANT TO BE MOAB, AND YET THEY END UP DOING EVERYTHING THEY CAN TO ENSURE THAT THEY WILL.

Can the communities surrounding the monument grab hold of their destinies before they get overrun? Scott Groene, who witnessed Moab's unchecked boom in the early 1990s, says wryly, "Everyone says they don't want to be Moab, and yet they end up doing everything they can to ensure that they will. Once the people show up who only want to make money, it's all over."

But Brad Barber is optimistic; he sees "an opportunity to create something great for southern Utah."

Pulling off Highway 12, I look out a seemingly endless expanse of domed, knobbed, and sculpted rock. Like a dark and gleaming serpent, a narrow ribbon of road winds miraculously through this desert. Beyond, the dark rising of the Henry Mountains.

A canyon wall seems close enough to touch. I pick up a stone and give it a good heave. It looks good for a while, riding high and strong, but then it slows and drops straight down, like Wile E. Coyote, into the abyss.

In this country, getting from here to there has never been easy.

April 14, 1997

TWO TALES OF A SINGLE COUNTY

Letter to the Editor

✿

DEAR HIGH COUNTRY NEWS,

In your recent article ("Beauty and the Beast," HCN, 4/14/97), Paul Larmer painted a rather bleak picture of the Kane County, Utah, economy. That negative economic portrait was part of an effort to explain why it was "no wonder everyone was hopping mad when the president took that hope (of the Andalex coal mine) away (by establishing the Grand Staircase-Escalante National Monument)." Larmer described the changes in the Kane County economy in the following terms:

"Not long ago, tourism was balanced by a substantial natural-resource-based economy. The scales tipped during the early 1990s, when Kanab lost more than 500 timber and uranium mining jobs. Families that had a primary breadwinner earning $20 to $30 an hour suddenly had to move or change occupations. Those who wanted to stay had to send Dad to work as a trucker or laborer in a distant city and add Mom, Grandma, and the kids to the work force, most often cleaning hotel rooms and flipping hamburgers for tourists at $5 an hour.

"In 1990, 1.5 people per Kane County household were in

the work force and the average income was $25,000, according to a recent economic report prepared for the county. Today, 2.6 people work per household and the average income has eroded to $18,000."

Unfortunately for your readers, Larmer stretched too far in providing an economic explanation for this anger over the establishment of the national monument. Every one of the quantitative factual statements made in this quote are grossly in error if they were intended to characterize the overall Kane County economy.

It would not have taken an economist to spot the exaggerations contained here. Some back-of-the-envelope arithmetic would have shown that these numbers simply could not be true. Consider the following:

These numbers imply that earnings per job (as opposed to earnings per household) fell from about $17,000 to about $7,000, a catastrophic crash to well below minimum-wage levels.

These numbers imply that an employment boom of major proportions took place in Kane County. To provide each of the growing number of households with 2.6 jobs, employment opportunities would have had to more than double, adding an additional 2,800 jobs to the economy.

These numbers imply that every man, woman, and child in Kane County, regardless of age and health, was "driven" into entering the workforce. The projected number of people per household in 1997 in Kane County was 2.8; apparently, fully 2.6 of them were actively employed in the commercial economy.

Kane County was gaining population through immigration, not losing it throughout this time period. People do not usually move towards economic catastrophe to work for less than minimum wage.

In addition, one might expect that regularly available state and federal data sources would have been consulted to see if these startling reported changes could be confirmed. State and federal data indicate the following:

In 1990, only one in 15 Kane County households earned the $50,000 per year implied by the $20-to-$30-per-hour wages cited. Such wages do not even remotely characterize a typical household.

PEOPLE DO NOT USUALLY MOVE TOWARDS ECONOMIC CATASTROPHE TO WORK FOR LESS THAN MINIMUM WAGE.

The jobs added in Kane County during the 1990s did not pay $5 per hour. The average annual wage in the expanding sectors, $16,300, was above the county-wide average, not below it, and is closer to $10 per hour.

Average incomes were rising significantly, not falling precipitously. Per capita income rose 33 percent in nominal terms and 15 percent in real purchasing power. The number of workers per household was declining modestly, not surging upward. This is what would be expected after major layoffs and before the economy can fully adjust.

This is not an attempt to paint a rosy picture of the Kane County economy. It has been through some wrenching shocks and some households have been badly hurt. The Kane County economy, however, has shown impressive vitality and resilience and can be expected to continue to do so.

How does one explain the startling contrast between the economic story that *High Country News* and local Kane County officials tell and the story that the economic statistics seem to tell? A good part of the answer, I suspect, lies in the fact that neither *High Country News* nor local officials like the economic changes that are taking place in the West. Their objections are not, however, economic. They are social and cultural. The new residents, the new businesses, the additional tourists, etc., carry with them values that the newspaper and Kane County officials do not much appreciate. Both wish that the land-based natural resource industries of the past could have prospered instead. Even if the new jobs paid good wages and provided stable employment, they would be objectionable on cultural and social terms.

These social critics, however, do not have the courage of their convictions. Instead of resting their case on their cultural and social objections, they wish also to show that the economic changes are causing economic decline. This is where things get confusing. Cultural objections that are legitimate and important to contemplate are restated in economic terms that are patently false. It is not clear that this helps inform the public dialogue.

If Kane County's residents and leaders are going to retain those things about their communities that are most important to them while adapting productively on their own terms where they have to, they need an accurate picture of where their economy is now and where it is heading.

Telling and re-telling false economic stories that reinforce their anger at the federal government and "outside" environmentalists does not equip them to protect what they want to protect.

Instead, it simply weakens and confuses them, making it more likely that they will face the outside pressures for change in a passive and helpless posture. *High Country News* is not doing them a favor by repeating uncritically these false economic stories. It is also not doing its readers a favor by reporting as economic facts what is primarily economic propaganda from the anti-environmental backlash.

THOMAS MICHAEL POWER
Missoula, Montana

PAUL LARMER RESPONDS:
Tom Power may be correct in his assertion that the employment numbers I used—and cited by county officials—are exaggerated. I should have been more careful before using them.

The economist who has worked on Kane County's economic plan, Gil Miller, says Power's information merits a closer look. But he cautions that it, too, may be skewed by the use of secondary sources. Miller says he is gathering new primary data from the county's citizens this summer that he hopes will shed more light on the county's economic condition. One thing he'll look at is distribution of wealth. A few wealthy individuals moving into the county could easily skew the average income figures for the county, he says.

But regardless of whether the numbers in my story are off, the reality of how people in Kane County feel about their community and the monument is not. The loss of 500 well-paying jobs is demoralizing to a community of 5,000 people, even if there is growth in other areas, and it can lead people to vent their frustration and anger against distant powers. In this case, the people vented against those who made the monument happen: the environmentalists and the Clinton administration.

I think this context is important for understanding how Kane County will deal with its future. But it's a context that Power makes only a passing attempt to understand. In his view, as long as the numbers look good overall, then everyone should be happy. Any community anger must be based not on economic factors, but rather on half-truths concocted by the anti-environmental backlash. Life isn't so simple.

If things are so great in this new economy, then why did southern Utah kick out Democratic Rep. Bill Orton and replace him with a conservative Republican? Why did hundreds of people wear black armbands and rally at the local gymnasium following the monument's creation? Was it all just a frenzy whipped up by the wise-use movement?

The Andalex coal mine and the jobs it promised may have been no more than a pipe dream—certainly many knowledgeable people have said that mining Kaiparowits coal would have been prohibitively expensive—but its loss still wounded people. They will get over it at some point, of course, and perhaps many will come to appreciate the monument as a far-sighted act of wisdom. But that's a story for the future.

The story now is about communities painfully adjusting to a new reality. And what I discovered is that people are adjusting. The leaders of Kane County, some of whom are newcomers, use the rhetoric of the anti-environmental crowd when it suits them, and they have sometimes acted out their anger in destructive ways (bulldozing roads, for instance). But they are by no means helpless victims. From what I can tell, they are trying to plot a course for their future, and the monument was the kick in the pants that got them started. That's what my story showed.

As for Power's swipes at HCN for wanting to return to the good old days of extraction, they just plain miss the mark. We try to present everyone's viewpoint, whether it comes from the mouth of an environmentalist or a bulldozing county commissioner. That makes some people—even the HCN staff—uncomfortable at times. But we hope that, in the long run, it leads to a better understanding of the human communities that populate the West.

A PROUD AND DEFIANT NATIVE

by Paul Larmer

⬳

THOUGH AS A CHILD SHE LIVED IN IDAHO and for a while in Tooele, Utah, Garfield County Commissioner Louise Liston has always considered her birthplace, Escalante, home. Before becoming a commissioner 10 years ago, Liston taught in a one-room school in the town of Boulder. Under her leadership, Garfield County has waged a rhetorical and legal battle against federal land agencies.

Louise Liston: "I love the land, and it's different from an environmentalist's love. We have a deep, abiding love; they have a weekend love affair. Their love is intense and passionate, but it's not an abiding love. That kind of love comes from making a living off the land. They go back to their amenities in their cities, while we continue to eke out an existence.

"I really think the president didn't know what he was doing when he created the monument. If he had visited the site, his perception would have been changed. He said, 'We can't have coal mines everywhere.' Well, that's right. We can only have mines where the coal is. Besides, the Kaiparowits is the ugliest place in the whole monument.

"But the monument is here and we've got to make something happen for the best. There are areas in the monument that deserve wilderness designation. In those places we could agree with environmentalists. But they want to drag the issue out for 70 years to keep their organizations going.

"We are already getting bombarded with visitors. Over Easter, the Hole-in-the-Rock road was bumper-to-bumper cars, and there were great clouds of dust. People were pulled off on all the side roads, and in the evening there were campfires everywhere. One couple in a Cadillac asked where they could climb the Grand Staircase. These people don't have any idea how rugged this country is. There will be accidents.

"Change is inevitable, but I think the land is going to be a victim. People will do a lot of damage that cattle and cowboys never did. You can't preserve the land and kick off the people. Rural values are the salvation of this country. I hate to see that go. We all do."

LETTER TO THE EDITOR

Dear *High Country News*,

I am offended by Louise Liston's statement, "I love the land, and it's different from an environmentalist's love. We have a deep, abiding love; they have a weekend love affair..." It is presumptuous to assume that other people's enjoyment of the nation's public lands is any less legitimate than one's own. Where I live and work, I am also surrounded by public lands. The forest and granite domes may be part of "my" backyard, but it is definitely not "mine."

That thousands of national forest visitors are happy to set up tents in nearby mosquito-laden campgrounds for a crowded holiday weekend of camping is no less valid and worthwhile than my walking explorations in wilderness. What matters most is that we all, each with our divergent views and backgrounds, work together to protect this precious heritage, and support the public agencies entrusted with land management.

My annual trip to Utah is a spiritual pilgrimage for me. I look forward to the lovely descending trill of the canyon wren, the smell of sagebrush, sunset glow on sandstone, and mysterious pictographs in hidden recesses. It is not required to reside on the land to legitimize one's respect for and appreciation of its values and beauty. Since much of our public lands are so fragile, it is best that most of us live elsewhere and just visit occasionally.

Once when I was guiding some international foresters on a walk in the Ancient Bristlecone Pine Forest—Inyo National Forest, California—an arboretum manager from Turkey stood apart from the group, his expression sad. Tears filled his eyes. He quietly said to me that he was overwhelmed by the extent and beauty of the American Western forests and parks, then added, "Most Americans do not know nor appreciate what they have. All they think about is exploiting the resource. If they are not careful, this all could become like Turkey, where we lost our forests hundreds of years ago."

I shall never forget his admonition.

JOAN BENNER
California

Bills Target Antiquities Act

by Emily Miller

~~

STILL SEETHING OVER President Clinton's creation of the 1.7 million-acre Grand Staircase-Escalante National Monument, Utah lawmakers are trying to turn their anger into law.

A bill co-sponsored by Utah Republican Senators Orrin Hatch and Bob Bennett would require the president to get approval from a state's governor and from Congress before establishing any monument over 5,000 acres. The proposal is one of several bills before Congress aimed at limiting the 91-year-old Antiquities Act, under which a fourth of all national monuments have been established.

"We're just trying to stop the president from doing whatever the heck he wants," says J.J. Brown, a Hatch staffer.

Another bill proposed by Sen. Bennett is designed to control management of the new monument, using Clinton's promises from his dedication speech as a guide. For example, Clinton said the monument "will remain open for multiple use including hunting, fishing, hiking, camping and grazing." Bennett's bill interprets this to mean the monument will be managed to serve "multiple use and sustained yield, including recreation, range, timber, minerals, oil and gas, watershed, wildlife, and natural, scientific, and historical values."

Environmental groups and Democrats in Congress oppose the legislation, saying that the Antiquities Act is important because it enabled the president to respond quickly to serious environmental threats, such as the Andalex coal mine, which was stopped by the creation of Utah's new monument.

In the House of Representatives, Utah Republican Jim Hansen is proposing a bill that would limit potential monuments to sites over 50,000 acres, a leap from the current 5,000-acre require-ment. So far, the bill has been defeated twice, but is being amended and will be reconsidered over the summer.

Al Eisenberg of the nonprofit National Parks and Conserva-tion Association believes that the legislation, as is, won't make it through the House. "Right now," he says, "it looks like we've built enough road blocks. They'll have a devil of a time coming over."

June 23, 1997

What's Underneath
the Staircase?

by Jamie Murray

ᴥ

On June 6, Conoco Inc., the largest subsidiary of DuPont
Corp., began drilling for oil on state school-trust lands within
the new Grand Staircase-Escalante National Monument. A second drilling rig stands at the head of Reese Canyon, in the monument's southern end, where the company plans to drill 14,000
feet into the earth's crust.

The Bureau of Land Management, which administers the
monument, says it can do nothing to stop Conoco because it has
no jurisdiction. The school-trust lands are "inholdings' managed
by Utah's School and Institutional Trust Lands Administration.
Although Utah's schools boast of large revenue returns from such
drilling, last year's royalties generated less than one-half of one
percent of Utah's total education budget, according to the
Southern Utah Wilderness Alliance (SUWA).

Conoco also holds leases on BLM land within the
monument's borders. But the leases were acquired before the
monument's creation, and the BLM says it can't deny drilling
there because the leases are "valid existing rights," says BLM
director Bill Lamb.

The agency could have delayed drilling by doing an environmental impact statement. Instead, it did a quicker environmental analysis in May 1997 and found that drilling "would not result in significant impacts on the human environment."

Conoco says it is waiting for results from its school-trust wells before deciding whether to drill on federal lands, according to company spokesman Bob Ireland.

Environmentalists are dismayed. "The BLM should put the leases on suspension to appropriately complete an EIS," says Pam Eaton of the Wilderness Society. SUWA agrees. "The BLM is proving itself unable to manage the monument," says spokesman Scott Groene, "and nobody seems willing to find a solution."

Environmental and citizens groups have rallied to protest the incursions, staging everything from vigils in Washington, D.C., to pickets in Salt Lake City. After the BLM, environmental groups, and Conoco met in February and failed to reach a compromise, Conoco announced it would begin drilling on a two-acre parcel of school-trust land.

BLM officials say privately they hope Conoco's wells on school-trust land will come up dry, forcing Conoco to abandon the area. Groene says unless the BLM makes a decisive move, "Conoco is going to keep on drilling."

Ruland Gill Jr., volunteer head of the state school-lands board and an executive with Questar (natural gas) Corp., said the clash is part of a larger effort to force the feds to deal with approximately 200,000 acres of school-trust land scattered throughout the monument. The state, Gill said in a speech in Park City in June, hopes to exert pressure on the federal government to discuss land trades.

Gill said the school lands outfit has been transformed over the past few years. Once accused by Utah's educators of being a good-old-boy outfit that didn't even have a balance sheet, the board now has a strategy for its lands and has accumulated a war chest to do legal battle with, or negotiate with, the federal government.

In 1993, the Congress passed Public Law 103-93, to trade or buy out another 200,000 acres of state inholdings in Arches, Capitol Reef, and other national parks and monuments in Utah. That process has led to lawsuits over the value of about 25 percent of the tracts, which is delaying completion of the tracks and buy-outs.

September 1, 1997

Utah's Bumbling Obscures
a Valid Complaint

by Jon Margolis

Now that government has become show business, one must classify political activities not according to ideology, party, or faction but by genre. Is the senator (president, governor, whatever) wearing the smiling comedy face today, or the gloomier mask of the drama?

Sometimes, though, there's little doubt, as is the case with the Utah congressional delegation's continuing fulminations over last year's declaration of the Grand Staircase-Escalante National Monument. This is comedy.

Nor are the congressmen alone. The delegation has a partner—the Utah Association of Counties, whose first lawsuit challenging the monument failed because papers were not served on the defendants in time. Probably they couldn't find where the president of the United States worked.

Undeterred, the association re-filed a suit almost certain to fail. This might not strike everyone in Utah as amusing. It's their money.

That's the trouble with comedy. It has this tendency to degenerate into farce, and to dance close to the line of bad taste.

Furthermore, comedy sometimes prevents the audience from seeing that the performers might have something serious to say.

The Utah House delegation has responded to the Grand Staircase-Escalante National Monument with three pieces of legislation. Rep. James Hansen introduced a bill that would limit all future designations to 5,000 acres. That would gut the act, but this is a measure filed for home-folk consumption, not for enactment into law.

The second proposal is a repeat of the minimalist version of a Utah wilderness bill that couldn't pass the last Congress. The sponsor here is Utah's new Republican congressman, Chris Cannon, who rode to victory last November on local opposition to the monument.

At a hearing on the bill, the comedy went sour. Among those testifying in opposition was Heidi McIntosh, the staff attorney for the Southern Utah Wilderness Alliance, and as he began to question her, Cannon asked not only her qualifications but also, "What is your religion?"

Restraining herself, Ms. McIntosh listed her qualifications and ignored the objectionable question, one that no one around Capitol Hill could remember being asked before, perhaps because even most congressmen have read the Constitution.

Well, Cannon is a newcomer, everyone is entitled to a mistake, and the next day he apologized to Ms. McIntosh. Whether the apology was inspired by the generally negative reaction at home provoked by a tape of the question being shown on Salt Lake City television is almost beside the point.

The delegation's showstopper is Hansen's Eastern Wilderness Bill, which would require the government to inventory all parcels of land in the East—federal, state or private—larger than 500 acres for possible inclusion in a wilderness system. This'll show all those Eastern snobs who try to tell Westerners what to do with their land by applying the provisions of the 1964 Wilderness Act to them. Well, more than applying, since the 1964 Wilderness Act called for looking at 5,000 acres of federal land—not private land.

But you never know what's going to happen when you start to fool around. What happened was that at a hearing on Hansen's bill on June 17, the Wilderness Society supported parts of it. Peter Kirby of the society's Atlanta office endorsed the idea of considering wilderness protection for some federal lands in the East.

> THIS'LL SHOW ALL THOSE EASTERN SNOBS WHO TRY TO TELL WESTERNERS WHAT TO DO WITH THEIR LAND BY APPLYING THE PROVISIONS OF THE 1964 WILDERNESS ACT TO THEM.

Meanwhile, back in Utah, there are lawsuits by the Western States Coalition, the Utah School and Institutional Trust Lands Administration, and the Association of Counties.

But maybe not all the counties. Salt Lake and Weber counties, where almost half of all Utahns live, have not committed themselves to helping pay the lawyers, a hesitation that may reflect a shift in public opinion. A poll taken by the *Salt Lake Tribune* in May found that a plurality of Utahns—and a majority in the two big counties—think the monument will be good for the state.

Or it may reflect a disinclination to throw good money at a lost cause. The basis for the action, according to the association's lawyer, Constance Brooks of Denver, is that the president's power to withdraw land from mineral entry was "repealed in 1976 by Section 204 of the Federal Land Policy and Management Act," commonly pronounced "flipma."

A POLL TAKEN BY THE SALT LAKE TRIBUNE IN MAY FOUND THAT A PLURALITY OF UTAHNS...THINK THE MONUMENT WILL BE GOOD FOR THE STATE.

But Section 204 doesn't say anything about repealing the Antiquities Act. It does deal with the same subject, giving rise to the argument that repeal is implied. The courts, however, don't like "repeal by implication." If Congress wants to repeal a law, it has to do so explicitly, as FLPMA in fact does to many laws.

The School Trust has the somewhat different, but no more likely to prevail, contention that the Antiquities Act was not designed as a land-management tool. However weak its legal case, the trust is trying to do its job, which is to gather as much money as possible for Utah's public schools.

And here we come to a serious point behind the comic fulminations. About 200,000 acres of the monument was land set aside at statehood (four sections out of every 36, statewide) to support Utah schools. Right now, they bring in only about one percent of the cost of public education, but there is a potential for more. All sides agree that there should be an equitable swap giving the school organization some valuable lands. What is going on now is a bargaining opener. If the Trust Administration is fairly compensated, spokesman David Hebertson said, "we'd have to drop the suit."

Bargaining also seems be what is going on between the feds and Conoco, which has an exploratory drill going on a state-owned parcel within the monument and has applied for permission to do the same on four federal parcels. The Bureau of Land Management seems likely to grant that permission in the hope that there isn't much oil there. If BLM is right, Conoco won't be in much of a bargaining position. If Conoco hits a big pool, the government will either have to let them drill or buy them off with some federal oil land elsewhere. That's not a joke.

And neither is everything about the anti-monument activity.

ONE CAN APPLAUD THE RESULTS OF THE GRAND STAIRCASE-ESCALANTE DESIGNATION AND STILL RETAIN SOME QUALMS ABOUT THE WAY IT WAS DONE.

One can applaud the results of the Grand Staircase-Escalante designation and still retain some qualms about the way it was done. It was, by any definition, a sweeping, if legal, exercise of executive power, always a cause for concern in a republic.

Nor was it a model of cooperative federalism. Consultation with the state was non-existent, and some reconsideration of the process would not be out of order.

Alas, serious matters cannot keep up with the comedy. One day in mid-July, the computer home page of the Association of

Counties was invaded by hackers who replaced the content with something written in German, or perhaps Swedish. The association reported this outrage to the FBI (yes, the FBI), and while it formally accused no one, it did point out that the incursion followed hard on a press conference it had held blasting the Southern Utah Wilderness Alliance, against which it is conducting something it calls a "SEWA-Watch" campaign.

Thus we may conclude with the most exalted of all forms of comedy. Up in New England where I live, when you say SEWA you're talking about a wastewater treatment facility.

September 1, 1997

Monumental Conflict Continues

by Paul Larmer

THE SAYING, "TIME HEALS ALL WOUNDS," may not apply to Utah, at least not to its politicians. Though more than a year has passed since President Clinton created the Grand Staircase-Escalante National Monument, the state's congressional delegation continues to try to dismantle it.

Republican Rep. Jim Hansen told the *Salt Lake Tribune* that memos recently subpoenaed from the White House show that the decision to create the monument was "strictly political" to help Clinton get elected and had nothing to do with the environment.

Outrage over how the monument was created, combined with pressure to exploit its minerals, means that "eventually (the monument) is going to be totally taken back…or Congress will have to go in there and change the boundaries," Hansen predicted.

The Utah delegation recently convinced the House of Representatives to pass legislation limiting the powers of the president to create national monuments. The bill, which passed October 7, 1997 on a partisan vote of 229–197, would change the 1906 Antiquities Act so that the president would need congressional approval to create monuments greater than 50,000 acres. The administration has promised a veto of the bill should it get by the Senate.

Environmentalists say the Utah delegation's fight has set a poor tone for the ongoing planning process for the monument, due for completion in 1999, and is out of touch with public opinion.

"I think people have left the politicians in the dust on this issue," says Scott Groene of the Southern Utah Wilderness Alliance. "While Hansen is screaming, people in southern Utah are figuring out how to live with the monument."

October 27, 1997

HAGGLING OVER THE GRAND STAIRCASE-ESCALANTE

by Greg Hanscom

✧

CONOCO HAS TURNED ITS BACK on an oil well in Utah's Grand Staircase-Escalante National Monument.

In December, Conoco engineers "packed up their oil rig and they are out of there," says Bureau of Land Management spokesman Don Banks. "The hole has been capped without a blade of monument grass or a dollar of taxpayer green being touched."

Conoco spokesman John Bennitt says the company decided not to drill on a federal lease in Reese Canyon after a test well on adjacent state school-trust lands failed to turn up producible oil. The federal lease expires February 8.

Although the focus has been on Conoco, the actual protagonists in what will probably be a long struggle are the federal government and the state agency that administers the 176,000 acres of Utah school-trust lands that lie within the 1.7 million-acre monument.

School-trust lands produce income for Utah's crowded schools. While a national constituency tries to protect the monument from mineral development, Utah educators and parents, liberals and conservatives alike, want to get the most out of the school-trust lands.

A Complex Craps Shoot

If Conoco walks away from its leases, the job of preserving the monument will be that much easier, or at least cheaper. If the company strikes it rich, state lands will be worth more—meaning more money for Utah's schools. So what has Conoco found?

"They did not find what they were looking for," says the BLM's Banks.

"It was the motherlode," says one official with the School and Institutional Trust Lands Administration.

There is reason for both claims. While the Reese Canyon well hit no oil, it did encounter natural gas in rock layers deep in the ground. Conoco says the gas was trapped too tightly in the stone to be worth pulling out, but it might indicate that there is oil or gas elsewhere in the monument.

In the coming months, Conoco says it will take a close look at its findings, and consider drilling a second well on one of the remaining 58 federal leases it signed before the monument's creation in 1996.

Right now, says the BLM's Don Banks, the state hasn't much of a case. "'The motherlode' is a bit of a stretch," he says. The state's claims are "purely speculative. No oil has been found yet." He expects that many of the remaining federal leases within the monument will expire when their 10-year life spans run out.

As the clock ticks on Conoco's federal leases, the state's need for a trade becomes more urgent. The school-trust parcels are small, and can only be developed as a part of a package that includes leases on surrounding federal lands. If the federal leases expire before the Trust Lands Administration can negotiate a trade, the board won't have much of a bargaining chip.

But the Interior Department has put negotiations on the back burner because the Trust Lands Administration is still trying to kill the monument with its lawsuit.

"It's awful difficult on one hand to be sued and on the other hand to be trying to work in good faith," says Banks.

The Trust Lands Administration faces a tough decision: Drop the lawsuit, concede that the monument is here to stay and work a trade with the BLM; or stand firm and hope that its lawsuit and pressure from Utah's congressional delegation will succeed in demolishing the monument.

> IT'S AWFUL DIFFICULT ON ONE HAND TO BE SUED AND ON THE OTHER HAND TO BE TRYING TO WORK IN GOOD FAITH.

At present, the Trust Lands Administration isn't budging. Its lawsuit may not reach the courts for months.

UTAH GETS TOUGH

As recently as 10 years ago, the Utah Trust Lands Administration would not have had the funds, the staff, or the tenacity to take on the federal government. Historically, it was controlled by members of the livestock, mining, and oil industries who stuck to business as usual.

"Practically every decision was rife with conflicts of interest," says Jon Souder, a professor at Northern Arizona University who has written extensively on state trust lands. "It was just untenable."

That changed in the late 1980s and early 1990s. A savvy group of college professors, academics, and leaders of the Utah

Education Coalition, Parent-Teacher Association and Utah Education Association lobbied the state legislature to force the board to make as much money as possible for Utah's schools.

Economist Margaret Bird, a school-trust lands expert with the Utah Office of Education, led the reform movement. She compares the Trust Lands Administration in its early days to an apartment complex in which the tenants decided how high their rent would be. Her job, she says, was to take back the school-trust lands from the tenants—the ranchers and miners and oilmen—and start "running it like a business."

Bird and her compatriots succeeded. Today, the Trust Lands Administration is run like a land development company. It still has a strong industry bias—the chairman of its seven-member board works for an oil company—but it now includes realtors, developers, and bankers.

The new Trust Lands Administration is tough. In 1993, Congress passed Public Law 103-93 to trade school-trust inholdings out of Arches, Capitol Reef, and other national parks and monuments in Utah. The administration agreed to sell or trade, but took the federal government to court last July, claiming the state was not getting enough out of the deals.

That case is still pending, but the School Trust's balance sheet shows that the new approach is working. In 1983, the state school fund contained $19 million, according to Bird. Today, it holds $164 million, and the program grossed $35 million last year alone. Although the increase is striking, school-trust lands still provide less than one percent of the state schools budget.

This new bulldog approach may be good for Utah's schools, but reform has complicated things. "We've always had the luxury of having these lands open," says Park City's director of public affairs Myles Rademan. "Now (the Trust Lands Administration) is more aggressive about getting into the development process."

Still, it is difficult to paint the Trust Lands Administration as just another anti-environmental Utah agency. "This is not some right-wing, anti-environmental thing," says Margaret Bird about the board's attitude toward the monument. "All we're saying is we need to get the most out of this for Utah's schoolchildren."

January 19, 1998

Monumental Deal Over Utah's Trust Lands

by Michelle Nijhuis

֍

ON MAY 8, after months of quiet negotiations, Utah Gov. Mike Leavitt and Secretary of the Interior Bruce Babbitt resolved a major sticking point in the debate over the Grand Staircase-Escalante National Monument. Their agreement trades the scattered blocks of state-owned school trust lands within the new monument for federal lands elsewhere in the state.

And, surprisingly, nearly everyone is satisfied with the deal. "This was the Achilles' heel of the monument, and major surgery has solved the problem," says Scott Groene of the Southern Utah Wilderness Alliance.

Brad Barber, the chief negotiator for the governor, says "It's a very fair deal for both sides, and a great deal for the parks and monuments of Utah." Under the broad agreement, the school trust lands within Utah's parks, monuments, Indian reservations, and most national forests—a total of nearly 377,000 acres—will be traded for a $50 million cash payment and 139,000 acres of federal land elsewhere in the state.

Utah politicians had decried the presidential establishment of the monument in late 1996, saying the designation would hurt the school trust—and Utah's public schools—by making it tougher to access and develop mining claims on the nearly 177,000 acres of state lands within the monument's boundaries.

As part of the deal, the State Institutional and Trust Lands Administration, the agency responsible for maximizing revenue from Utah's school trust lands, will drop two lawsuits against the federal government. The first, filed last July, said the Department of Interior had not followed Public Law 103-93, a 1993 federal law requiring trade-outs for state inholdings in Utah's parks, monuments, national forests, and reservations. The second challenged the designation of the new monument, arguing that it reduced earnings from mining and grazing on trust lands.

The state agency proposed a swap of its holdings in the monument about a year ago, says Dave Hebertson of the Trust Lands Administration. During negotiations between the governor's staff and the Department of the Interior, the agreement was expanded to include almost all of the state inholdings and address both lawsuits.

Environmental groups were not a part of the agreement, but they were consulted throughout the process. Lawson LeGate of the Utah chapter of the Sierra Club says the Trust Lands Administration "has been very good about meeting with us to consider tracts of lands they'd like to acquire. They recognize that the support of the Utah environmental community is a key to the success of this effort."

"I think they were impressed that we cared enough to ask," says Hebertson. All of the lands acquired by the state have potential mineral or development value, but none of them are under consideration for wilderness status.

Utah's congressional delegation is also backing the agreement, which is expected to come before the House and Senate for a vote before the end of the legislative session next month. Under Public Law 103-93, the $50 million payment to the state will be obtained from royalties on federal coal leases in Utah.

The deal may have implications beyond the monument. The Utah Wilderness Coalition's proposal for 5.7 million acres of Bureau of Land Management land in Utah—now a congressional bill—also contains a checkerboard of state lands, and critics of the bill have long invoked the welfare of Utah schoolchildren.

> WE'RE NOT OPPOSED TO WILDERNESS. WE'RE JUST OPPOSED TO PAYING FOR IT.

"There's no question that this will open up a lot of new doors," says Barber. "If wilderness legislation does move forward, we now have a framework to do similar exchanges."

And if the bill specified a similar swap of the state's holdings within wilderness areas, says Hebertson, his agency would stop fighting the proposal. "The only issue in my mind is fair market values," he says. "We're not opposed to wilderness. We're just opposed to paying for it."

May 25, 1998

GREENS NOT WELCOME
IN ESCALANTE

by Brent Israelsen

⚶

HEAVY MACHINERY ROLLED into Escalante, Utah the week of April 12. Construction was imminent on the $7.5 million New Wide Hollow Reservoir that would provide water for a couple dozen ranchers in this rural southern Utah town.

Then, on April 15, under pressure from environmentalists who say the reservoir would harm the Escalante River, the Bureau of Land Management put the project on hold. That night, someone re-arranged an irrigation pipe on the property of Patrick Diehl and Tori Woodward, recent arrivals from California who have opposed the reservoir. A valve was opened and 32,000 gallons of water gushed into a hole the couple had recently dug for a shop and studio.

The couple reported the incident to the police but has received little sympathy from locals. Instead, a week later, the New Escalante Irrigation Company sent Diehl and Woodward a notice that the "open pipe" that flooded their excavation was a violation of company rules, and they would have to pay a $1,150 fine.

The sabotage is just one sign that tensions are rising in this ranching town, population 1,200, which is struggling to adjust to life with a national monument in its back yard, and conservationists pushing to set aside more of the landscape as wilderness.

"They need a better grip on Escalante's background, customs and culture," Escalante Mayor Lenza Wilson says of green-leaning newcomers. "The jury (of local opinion) has returned a very strong verdict, and they are not welcome here."

An Unenviable Position

The New Escalante Irrigation Co. currently draws water from the Wide Hollow Reservoir, which has filled with so much silt in the past few years that it can hold just 1,000 acre-feet of water. An acre-foot is 325,851 gallons. It takes about 5 acre-feet of water to grow a season's worth of alfalfa on an acre of land in Escalante. By July or August, the irrigation company is usually out of water.

The proposed New Wide Hollow Reservoir would provide an additional 6,100 acre-feet of water, which the irrigation company says would be used to grow alfalfa. "That reservoir is our lifeline," said irrigation company water master Pat Coughlin. "Our livelihood depends on our water storage."

THAT RESERVOIR IS OUR LIFELINE.... OUR LIVELIHOOD DEPENDS ON OUR WATER STORAGE.

But wilderness advocates argue that the new reservoir would dry up a creek and disrupt the flow of the Escalante River. On April 11, Patrick Diehl criticized the dam in the *Salt Lake Tribune* for its potential to harm the river ecosystem downstream. He also suggested that the irrigation company wanted the extra water not for agriculture but for more lucrative residential development.

To Escalante residents, it was the final insult. "I'm a man of few words, and when I speak, they are real harsh," said Barry Barnson, a 31-year Escalante resident and member of the irrigation company's board. "The thing that got Patrick Diehl in trouble is he took the route that we're a bunch of idiots."

Barnson and other irrigation company board members have implied that Diehl and Woodward are responsible for the errant water, either through negligence or as a publicity stunt. They insist that fines like the one levied against the pair are common. But Diehl insists that he and Woodward are the victims of vandalism, which will cost them $500 to repair. Garfield County Deputy Sheriff Monte Luker sides with the couple, saying, "I feel it was a vandalism and do not think (Diehl and Woodward) were involved."

Diehl plans to appeal the fine, but he will be in the unenviable position of pleading his case before a board composed of people who would have benefited from the reservoir he opposed. Outraged at how Diehl and Woodward have been treated, the Southern Utah Wilderness Alliance has agreed to provide an attorney.

TENSIONS RISE OVER WILDERNESS

Wilderness advocates, too, have been feeling unwelcome in Escalante lately. On April 23, the Bureau of Land Management held a public open house at the local high school to discuss the agency's plan to add federal lands to the inventory of wilderness study areas.

Representing the Utah Wilderness Coalition at the meeting was Bob Walton of Salt Lake City. Walton displayed stacks of wilderness literature and bumper stickers in the lobby.

A man wearing a large hat grabbed the stickers, cut them in half with a big hunting knife and threw them in a garbage can. The man said something to the effect of, "This is garbage. We won't have any of this here," says Walton.

A short time later, Walton put out more literature and bumper stickers. The man returned and destroyed them in the same manner.

"Soon after that, a rather large group of folks began to gather around me, verbally harassing and threatening me," Walton wrote in a report to the Escalante police. "One person said, 'We ought to kill you.'"

Walton retreated into the meeting and asked agency officials for an escort to his car. "It's a real shame. I feel like I have to watch my back in Escalante. That's disheartening because it's a place I love," said Walton, a sixth-generation Utahn.

WILDERNESS ADVOCATES...HAVE BEEN FEELING UNWELCOME IN ESCALANTE LATELY.

Another Garfield County environmental activist is searching for middle ground between old-timers and newcomers. Mark Austin, who owns the Boulder Mountain Lodge in Boulder, is working with farmers and wilderness advocates to come up with an environmentally sensitive design for the New Wide Hollow Reservoir.

The Wilderness Society and the Southern Utah Wilderness Alliance are willing to consider a compromise if it includes enough environmental safeguards. And irrigation company officials say they are willing to talk, but they suspect that environmentalists will ask for too many concessions. "The scuttlebutt is what they want to do is trade the reservoir for us backing off our opposition to additional wilderness," Wide Hollow Water Conservancy District member Dal Liston told the *Salt Lake Tribune*, "which is definitely not something we would do."

May 24, 1999

IS THE GRAND STAIRCASE-ESCALANTE A MODEL MONUMENT?

by Paul Larmer

≪⅊

THREE YEARS AGO, Jerry Meredith was pretty sure he had landed one of the toughest jobs in the federal government. The 51-year-old middle manager for the Bureau of Land Management had just been tagged to oversee the brand-new Grand Staircase-Escalante National Monument.

Many conservationists were skeptical that Meredith's agency, the BLM—derisively called the "Bureau of Livestock and Mining" by some—was capable of managing a national monument, a task traditionally handed to the National Park Service. Throw on top of that continuing local resentment of the monument and a rigid deadline—the presidential decree gave the Interior Department three years to come up with a management plan—and Meredith could see the makings of a failure.

"My first thought was, 'No way, this can't be done,'" recalls Meredith. "I had no employees, no budget, not even an office."

But done it he has. Bolstered by a Clinton administration intent on making the monument a model of success, Meredith's team of 20 scientists and policy makers has finished a management plan that will likely be signed by U.S. Secretary of the

Interior Bruce Babbitt by the end of the year, capping a remarkable three years of on-the-ground conservation accomplishments in southern Utah.

Significant pockets of dissent remain. Meredith's office has received nearly 100 letters protesting portions of the new plan, and the monument is still under a legal challenge from the Utah Association of Counties. But Meredith says the BLM has weathered the storm quite nicely, and shown that it can manage a world-class resource while still accommodating local uses, such as cattle grazing and wood collection.

> THE MONUMENT IS BEING HELD UP AS THE MODEL. THE QUESTION: IS IT A GOOD ONE OR A BAD ONE?

As Bruce Babbitt zeroes in on protecting other ecologically significant public lands in the West, perhaps through further use of executive orders under the Antiquities Act of 1906, the monument is being held up as the model. The question: Is it a good one or a bad one?

MUTED PRAISE

A good model, would be the answer from most environmentalists, though they see flaws in the new management plan.

"We have some problems with the grazing and off-road vehicle provisions, but the BLM did a pretty good job (with the management plan)," says Heidi McIntosh, a lawyer with the Southern Utah Wilderness Alliance, an organization that has often been at odds with the BLM. "The agency took a fairly protective stance to protect the primitive character of the land."

The BLM's preferred management option calls for 65 percent of the monument, or 1.2 million acres, to be protected as a primitive zone, with no visitor facilities and extremely limited motorized access.

What development takes place will occur in the communities surrounding the monument, an approach that has drawn muted praise from local leaders. Next year bulldozers will begin clearing land for visitor centers in Big Water, Glendale, and Cannonville. And Kanab is close to securing a contract for constructing the monument headquarters building, which it plans to lease back to the federal government, as part of a large, centrally located "city heritage plaza."

"The community is excited about this," says Kanab mayor Karen Alvey. "It will help make us a destination point for visitors and give them a reason to stay for two or three days instead of just passing through."

The headquarters will also bring a sizeable payroll—as many as 35 federal employees will work out of Kanab.

"The creation of the monument is still a real sore subject around here," says Alvey. "But we're trying to make lemonade out of lemons."

Meredith says his agency has won the support of both locals and Salt Lake City environmentalists. "We've gone out of our way to listen to people and be accessible through this process, and we're proud of what we've come up with," he says. "How many federal planning projects do you know that come in on time and under budget?"

BIG BUCKS SMOOTH THE WATERS

It helps, of course, if you have a sizeable budget and firm backing from your bosses. From the start, the monument planning effort has been a first-class operation. Meredith was able to draw on the best talent throughout the nation to create his planning "dream team," choosing from other federal and state agencies. In a concession to Utah, the Clinton administration let Gov. Mike Leavitt appoint five members to the team.

"When you call the planning team, things actually get done," says Joro Walker, a lawyer who, on behalf of environmental groups, has protested sections of the monument plan dealing with grazing and ORV use. "That's definitely unique."

"They have included local communities to a very large extent," echoes Mike Jenel, a planning consultant working for Kane County.

> WE'VE GONE OUT OF OUR WAY TO LISTEN TO PEOPLE AND BE ACCESSIBLE THROUGH THIS PROCESS, AND WE'RE PROUD OF WHAT WE'VE COME UP WITH.

Meredith doesn't deny that a quality staff and plenty of money have been important to the completion of the management plan, but he says the monument's budget is not extravagant. It ran just under $2 million in 1998, he says, nearly half a million below what Congress allocated.

Does the BLM have the resources to manage the other significant sites in the West being eyed by Interior Secretary

Bruce Babbitt? Meredith says the agency has already invested heavily in places like the California Desert and the Columbia River Basin and could probably put together competent planning teams at a reasonable cost in other places.

"We have a tradition of frugality," he says. "But we are willing to put out resources where it is necessary."

THE EXTRA EFFORT

The Clinton administration's investment in the Grand Staircase-Escalante National Monument has gone well beyond planning monies, however. This fall it closed a deal buying out leases held by Andalex, the coal company that wanted to develop a mine on the Kaiparowits Plateau. If Congress approves the expenditure, U.S. taxpayers will pay Andalex $14 million in cash in exchange for 34,499 acres of federal coal leases in the monument.

And last year, the Interior Department and the state of Utah sat down and hammered out an agreement that gives Utah $50 million and 139,000 acres of federal land in exchange for scattered state-owned school trust lands throughout the state, including those in the monument.

"The real story here is what an agency like the BLM can accomplish when it is given adequate resources," says Bill Hedden, Utah representative for the Grand Canyon Trust, a conservation group based in Flagstaff, Ariz. "This monument is now becoming a full-fledged monument, irrespective of which agency is managing it."

Hedden has had a hand in the monument's maturation. Over the past year he has worked out deals with several ranchers and the BLM to move cattle out of the monument and permanently retire federal grazing allotments in environmentally sensitive areas.

The creation of the monument was the catalyst for the ranchers, Hedden says. The ranchers believed there would be more scrutiny of their activities by the agency and the public, and that they would eventually be regulated out of business.

"Combine that with the collapse of the beef market and you can see why they think this is the time to sell out," he says.

HEAVY HAND OR GUIDING LIGHT?

Of course, not everyone is happy. The Utah Association of Counties still has a lawsuit in federal court challenging the legality of the monument itself. It claims the president exceeded his authority under the Antiquities Act.

Most observers say the lawsuit is a longshot, but the possibility of a court victory has kept resistance alive.

Last summer, Kane County commissioners were on the verge of signing an agreement with the BLM that would finally resolve the contentious issue of which roads the county owns within the new monument. Under heavy pressure from the local chapter of People for the USA, a national "wise use" organization, the commissioners backed off.

The dissent is proof that many local citizens still haven't bought into the monument, says Ken Sizemore, deputy director of the Five Counties Association of Government in southern Utah. Sizemore, who until last summer was the community leader for the monument planning team, appointed by Gov. Leavitt, says he sees a "groundswell" of opposition to the monument bubbling up as the management plan nears completion.

"While the elected officials were conversant in the planning process and bought into it, the general citizenry was still very upset," says Sizemore.

The persistent political opposition to the monument has convinced Bruce Babbitt to take a new tack. Babbitt has said that places such as the Arizona Strip, north of the Grand Canyon, and Steens Mountain in southeastern Oregon, deserve protection. Let the locals come up with a protection plan. If they don't, he adds, he'll ask the administration to unleash the Antiquities Act.

Sizemore says the new approach is as draconian as the old one. "The administration is making the same mistake with these new areas," he says. "Sure, it would be great to have a local, legislative proposal drive the process, but when you get down to brass tacks, the administration opposes the concepts and precepts embodied in locally produced legislation."

Monument manager Meredith says some locals will always be unhappy because "there is a general dislike in the rural West for anything that's perceived to limit the ability to make money from natural resource development." Sometimes direction from on high is not a bad thing, he says, especially when there is little prospect of consensus at the local level.

"The president's proclamation for the monument clearly defines what we can and cannot do," says Meredith. "And that has been helpful."

November 22, 1999

RANCHERS TAKE LAW INTO THEIR OWN HANDS

by Tim Sullivan

꧁

WHAT BEGAN AS the Bureau of Land Management's attempt to salvage rangeland from a dry summer has become a miniature Sagebrush Rebellion.

This summer, the BLM repeatedly ordered ranchers Quinn Griffin and Mary Bulloch to remove their cattle from remote grazing allotments in Grand Staircase-Escalante National Monument. Finally, the agency did the deed itself, impounding 44 cows in a Salina, Utah, feedlot to await auctioning.

Griffin, Bulloch, and about 14 other ranchers were quick to retaliate, however. On Election Day, the ranchers took back the cattle after convincing Sevier County attorney Don Brown that they owned the animals.

"Since when did the cattle become government property?" asks Todd Macfarlane, a rancher and lawyer representing a few of the ranchers involved. Macfarlane says the ranchers had every right to take back their herds and did so in a forthright, peaceful manner. It was the BLM, he says, that violated the law.

U.S. attorney Paul Warner is threatening the ranchers with $250,000 fines and 10 years in prison if they don't return the cattle. Whether or not the BLM had the right to impound the cows, adds Warner's spokeswoman, Melodie Rydalch, stealing them back wasn't the answer.

"If they had a grievance," says Rydalch, "the remedy for that is to go to court and tell the BLM they were wrong."

While Macfarlane and Rydalch confirm that the U.S. attorney is close to a deal with Griffin, Mary Bulloch, the rancher who owns most of the cattle, is far from giving in.

Bill Hedden of the Grand Canyon Trust finds the whole situation disheartening. If the BLM wasn't within the law in impounding the cows, says Hedden, then "they'd better forget about having any authority to manage grazing" on the monument in the future.

December 4, 2000

ACT III

❦

FROM ONE TO MANY

Silver Falls Creek in Grand Staircase-Escalante National Monument

PHOTO CREDIT: JACK MCLELLAN

INTERIOR VIEW III

by Ed Marston

⁓

MARSTON: Looking at all the new monuments…were these part of an overall strategy?

BABBITT: Well, it's Clinton-style governance, which means that it would be an overstatement to say that it is tidy, with uniform lines, authority, and delegation. That said, I think there are some common strands, certainly in terms of the use of the Antiquities Act. You know, that has been driven from the Interior Department, and with some fairly clear ideas of the importance and priorities….

MARSTON: You've gotten a lot of credit for the monuments. Did that get the White House angry at you?

BABBITT: Well, this stuff is complicated. Let me just say that in all the bureaucratic intrigue which always is worse at the White House staff level, my friendship with Gov. Bill Clinton, I think, made a difference.

MARSTON: From back when you were (Arizona) Gov. Bruce Babbitt?

BABBITT: Yeah. There's no question that my personal relationship helped. It didn't make me an insider. But the important thing was that when I really wanted to start to drive a message, I had the appropriate amount of access. And I'm very grateful for that.

GO TELL IT ON THE MOUNTAIN

by Stephen Stuebner

ⅇ

ATOP 9,600-FOOT STEENS MOUNTAIN in eastern Oregon, a brisk northwest wind races up the spectacular U-shaped canyon of Little Blitzen Creek at dawn. Howling over the top of golden aspen trees in the canyon below, the wind rips up-canyon to a steep alpine bowl at the top of the draw, and—poof!—like magic, creamy clouds form at the summit.

For a moment, the clouds cling to the edge of a mile-high cliff. But the force of the roaring gale hurls them into a void above the Alvord Desert, where they vanish.

The gusts seem appropriate on this crisp fall morning, since the winds of change are blowing with a fury on Steens Mountain. Right now, the 900,000-acre mountain is a relatively well-kept secret, managed by the Bureau of Land Management under no official label. But in August, Interior Secretary Bruce Babbitt visited nearby Burns, the heart of Oregon cattle country, and there he announced that he intends to protect the mountain as a federal treasure.

"We're thrilled," says Bill Marlett, executive director of the Oregon Natural Desert Association, a group that has long advocated national park status for the Steens. His group now backs a national monument designation—as long as 18,000 cattle and 35 ranchers are yanked off the mountain by a massive government buyout.

At least 30 percent of the mountain is privately owned— about 232,000 acres. At $1,000 an acre, a buyout would cost $232 million.

Babbitt has a different vision. The secretary has pledged to preserve ranching in the Steens, meaning that he'll help ranchers keep their inholdings. And Steens ranchers, who have improved stewardship on the mountain and who provide free access to campers, anglers, and hunters, want to stay.

"Basically, our ranch isn't for sale," says Stacy Davies, manager of the Roaring Springs Ranch, the largest on the mountain. "In my life, I have a vision of making a ranch a model for ecological stewardship and economic sustainability. This is a ranch where that can work. It would be just heartbreaking to have that vision destroyed."

IN MY LIFE, I HAVE A VISION OF MAKING A RANCH A MODEL FOR ECOLOGICAL STEWARD-SHIP AND ECONOMIC SUSTAINABILITY. THIS IS A RANCH WHERE THAT CAN WORK.

Babbitt has promised that the Clinton administration will not make the Steens an instant national monument, as it did prior to the 1996 election with the Grand Staircase-Escalante National Monument in southern Utah. "I'm not going to pull off some kind of surprise while everyone is eating their

Christmas turkey," he says. Instead, he gave a local agency advisory committee two months to craft a legislative plan for a national conservation area at Steens Mountain. If they don't reach an agreement, Babbitt hinted, Clinton will create a Steens National Monument in election year 2000.

BIG-LEAGUE POLITICS WILL HOVER LIKE A TURKEY VULTURE OVER THE STEENS FOR THE NEXT YEAR.

Big-league politics will hover like a turkey vulture over the Steens for the next year, as Babbitt seeks to enhance his legacy, improve the chances for Democratic presidential candidate Al Gore, and carve out Clinton's place in history. The Steens fight will also test Babbitt's longtime support of local decision-making. At this lonely Great Basin landmark, he'll find out if those who know the mountain best can preserve it for the nation.

A STORMY MONUMENT

Steens Mountain looms like a towering icon in the open landscape, its snow-streaked rocky brow reaching higher than any other mountain between the Cascades and the Northern Rockies.

Basalt and rhyolite lava flows formed the geologic core of the Steens about eight million years ago. The flows inscribed dramatic brown and red horizontal bands and vertical columns on the mountain's flanks. Later, the 65-mile-long mountain rose in a great tilt from the Alvord Desert. With each earthquake episode, the mountain grew taller and the valley dropped in elevation. Glaciers put a finishing touch on the west slope of the Steens, carving out 10 U-shaped canyons that flow toward the Malheur National Wildlife Refuge.

Babbitt was entranced with the Steens after an overflight with Oregon Gov. John Kitzhaber in August. "It's the only place I've seen where you have alpine glacial valleys end in the desert," he said. "I was impressed with the whole area, (the) high alpine country adjacent to a national wildlife refuge with exceptional diversity and importance."

Seven streams on the west slope form the Donner und Blitzen River—German for "thunder and lightning"—so named by German immigrants for the mountain's stormy moods. A 56-mile loop of gravel road provides jaw-dropping scenic views, from aspen and cottonwood-lined creeks to knots of mountain mahogany on windswept ridges to alpine meadows and rocky peaks at the summit.

The Bureau of Land Management estimates that most of the 30,000 people who visit the Steens each year drive and camp along the loop road. The more hardy cross the Steens on the Desert Trail, a 150-mile hiking route from the Pueblo Mountains at the Nevada border to Riddle Mountain, southeast of Burns.

Hunters chase sage grouse, chukar partridge, elk, mule deer, antelope and bighorn sheep in the fall. Anglers pursue redband trout.

"It's danged fun to go fish for redbands," says rancher Davies. "We catch 18-inchers in Skull Creek." In the Alvord Desert, Mann Creek Reservoir is a magnet for anglers seeking hefty hybrid Lahontan cutthroats. Alvord Hot Springs, covered by a dented tin shack riddled with bullet holes, is a popular stop for campers and birders.

The Steens provides a refuge for the coveted Kiger mustangs and several other wild horse herds. At BLM roundups, Kigers can fetch up to $13,000 because some believe they can be traced to ancient Spanish bloodlines.

Another unique characteristic: At least eight plants found nowhere else in the Great Basin reside on Steens Mountain. Donald Mansfield, a biology professor at Albertson College of Idaho in Caldwell, says the plants suggest that the range was linked to the Sierra Nevada and Northern Rockies in earlier times.

"It's a stepping stone, really, between the two ranges," Mansfield says. "The plants are telling us something about the land connections in the Pleistocene era, but we don't know many details."

Mansfield has written a letter to the Burns BLM, urging it to protect rare plants from cows and people, no matter what kind of new designation the Steens receives. "Here you've got something so unique, botanically, that I'd hate to see it wrecked any more before we know what we've got," he says.

> HERE YOU'VE GOT SOMETHING SO UNIQUE, BOTANICALLY, THAT I'D HATE TO SEE IT WRECKED ANY MORE BEFORE WE KNOW WHAT WE'VE GOT.

THE POLITICAL LANDSCAPE

For decades, environmentalists have pushed for more protection for Steens Mountain. Sen. Mark O. Hatfield, R-Ore., requested a national park study in the 1960s. In 1991, Hatfield and then-

Sen. Bob Packwood, R-Ore., introduced a proposal for a national conservation area, and Rep. Bob Smith, R-Ore., sponsored a competing proposal. Neither passed Congress.

So Babbitt's proposal for a BLM-managed national conservation area may be the best chance yet to safeguard the Steens. While national parks operate under a strict set of general regulations, the management of national conservation areas can vary widely. With this flexibility in mind, Babbitt had called for the 15-member BLM Southeast Oregon Resource Advisory Council to come up with a general plan for a Steens National Conservation Area by October 15, including a wilderness proposal and a grazing management plan.

The Resource Advisory Council (RAC) model is Babbitt's brainchild. Established early in his tenure, the councils include ranchers, outfitters, environmental groups, tribal representatives and other community members, and they're designed to increase local participation in BLM decisions.

Yet he handed the Southeast Oregon council a job of national proportions. It could effect big changes on Steens Mountain, says Miles Brown, BLM field manager for the Andrews Resource Area in Burns. The amount of wilderness that could be established in the area is "wide open," he says, and a conservation area designation might help the agency secure Land and Water Conservation Fund monies to buy some of the scattered private parcels.

But at an October 27 meeting with Babbitt, held at a cozy dining-room table in the Sage Country Inn Bed and Breakfast in Burns, the committee submitted a three-page report opposing a new designation for the Steens. While many groups and individuals from western and central Oregon supported a national monument or large-scale wilderness area, said the report, most local landowners were hostile to tougher protection.

WHILE MANY GROUPS AND INDIVIDUALS FROM WESTERN AND CENTRAL OREGON SUPPORTED A NATIONAL MONUMENT OR LARGE-SCALE WILDERNESS AREA, MOST LOCAL LANDOWNERS WERE HOSTILE TO TOUGHER PROTECTION.

Advisory council chairman Mike Golden, a retired biologist, also reported that the committee needed more time to wrestle with the wilderness question.

"There's no question about it—wilderness is the diciest issue," he says. "The other difficult one is grazing, how much and where."

It wasn't the outcome Babbitt might have hoped for, but he prodded the group to continue negotiations. "This report is right on in terms of my understanding of the land and your concerns," he told the group. "We ought to set up a process where we can determine what we agree on, and what disagreements remain."

The committee agreed to form a small group of five to seven people to work on the outlines of a legislative plan with Gov. Kitzhaber and with Rep. Greg Walden, R-Ore., who represents Harney County and rural Oregon. Eventually, Babbitt said, all Oregon senators and congressmen must support the bill.

"We've got to have them all," he said. "The climate in Washington is such that anybody can block anything." He promised to return in January to check on progress and help citizens hammer out a deal.

Babbitt convinced the committee that a legislative plan crafted by Oregon people would be preferable to letting outsiders decide what's right for Steens Mountain. If they can come up with a plan, "any talk of the

THE CLIMATE IN WASHINGTON IS SUCH THAT ANYBODY CAN BLOCK ANYTHING.

Park Service taking over this area will be off the table for several generations," he said. His veiled threat was answered by a round of knowing smiles.

THE HOLDOUTS

But the committee hasn't been talking about turning the area over to the Park Service, and it's not talking about ending grazing on the Steens. Babbitt's loyalty to the BLM and his commitment to keeping ranchers in business have tempered the initial enthusiasm of some environmentalists.

"They're never going to deliver what we want," Bill Marlett says of the BLM.

"If this designation amounts to just changing pretty colors on a map, we won't support it," says Wendell Wood, the Oregon Natural Resources Council's southern field representative in Klamath Falls. "This is literally the crown jewel in Oregon's high desert. To us, it's a no-brainer. Any kind of protection that doesn't eliminate livestock grazing, off-road vehicles, and mining is really no protection at all."

"Cows can graze just about everywhere in eastern Oregon,"

says Alice Elshoff, an Oregon Natural Desert Association board member based in Frenchglen. "We think there're some places that shouldn't have cows."

Neither the Oregon Natural Resources Council nor the Natural Desert Association are participating in the negotiations.

Other environmentalists have more hope for the effort. Jill Workman, who represents the Sierra Club on the council, believes that a solution could include continued grazing.

> WE THINK THERE ARE SOME PLACES THAT SHOULDN'T HAVE COWS.

"The Sierra Club has a long history of working things out with the cattle industry," she says. "It's not going to be something that both sides really love, but hopefully we'll be able to live with it."

She says some ranchers have worked hard to protect streambanks from overgrazing, and she salutes Stacy Davies for signing conservation agreements with the U.S. Fish and Wildlife Service to protect redband trout.

"The owner of Roaring Springs Ranch is an avid fisherman and hunter. He really wants to do what's right for fish and wildlife," Workman says.

Rancher Fred Otley, who organized Friends of Steens Mountain to ensure that private landowners get a fair shake, says ranchers will have to be good stewards to remain on the mountain. "We've worked really hard to manage livestock in a progressive manner," he says. "We've got proof with photos and documentation."

The ranchers also have the support of Gov. John Kitzhaber, who's expected to help shepherd any new designation. "It's not a rational position to talk about buying out the ranchers," says Peter Green, senior natural resources aide for Kitzhaber. "I don't see that as a realistic or necessary solution."

But the council members have to do more than agree among themselves. Any legislation that includes grazing is sure to draw criticism from hardline environmentalists, and they're aware of their political power.

"If environmentalists don't hail it as a great thing, if we say, 'This is crap,' then the administration doesn't get as many points," says Andy Kerr, who represents The Wilderness Society on the Steens Mountain issue. "Babbitt is trying to take livestock grazing off the table, but we're not going to let him."

AT WHAT PRICE?

Many people in Oregon question what may be gained—or lost—by a new classification for the Steens. Locals fear the "Yosemite syndrome" may lead to more visitors, more paved roads, more law enforcement, and less primitive character for this relatively unknown place. And if ranchers and private property owners are angry with the results of Babbitt's proposal, barbed-wire fences and no-trespassing signs could go up on private land in a hurry.

Cindy Witzel runs Steens Mountain Packers with her husband, John, who grew up on a ranch in the Steens. They guide summer horseback riding trips, elk-hunting trips, bird-hunting trips, and backcountry ski adventures. "Yeah, we stand to gain, but it'll change this area forever," Witzel says. "We'd rather see no designation."

Even the liberal *Register-Guard* in Eugene and *The*

Oregonian in Portland have editorialized against Babbitt's plan.

"Solitude is Steens Mountain's most fragile feature," the *Register-Guard* editorial said. "A caravan of RVs making its dusty way from Fish Lake Road to the summit will have a greater effect on Steens Mountain than a herd of cattle in Kiger Gorge."

SOLITUDE IS STEENS MOUNTAIN'S MOST FRAGILE FEATURE.

Although Babbitt says his proposal for the Steens "really isn't about legacy," history judges Interior secretaries by the national treasures they protect from the long arm of development—and the controversies they brave to do it. Think of Stewart Udall and Cecil Andrus; they made their mark with a bevy of national parks, wilderness areas, and monuments, all of which faced local opposition.

"If you look back at nearly every national monument in this country," says Kerr, "the locals fought it and hated the idea, but they were rolled by the greater national interest."

Babbitt believes this bitterness can be avoided. By giving locals a chance to chart the future of the Steens and other areas around the West, he hopes to convince them that new, tougher protections are necessary. If his approach works, he could leave a different—some might say happier—legacy than his predecessors. And if it doesn't? Unless he wants his proposals to vanish like the clouds on Steens Mountain, he'll have to be willing to take the heat.

"The future is coming at us," he says. "We have to get out ahead of the game and protect these areas before it's too late."

November 22, 1999

Babbitt Looks for Support on His Home Turf

by Tim Westby

˞ℓℓ

THE SHIVWITS PLATEAU wasn't on environmentalists' radar screen a year ago. Better known as the Arizona Strip, the Shivwits lies in the extreme northwestern corner of Arizona. Cut off from the rest of the state by the Grand Canyon and the Colorado River, it is a region of sagebrush flats, pinon-juniper forests, and deep canyons that only mule deer hunters and a handful of ranchers seemed to care about.

That changed last November, when Department of Interior Secretary Bruce Babbitt, a northern Arizona native, proposed greater federal protection for a 550,000-acre swath of federal lands bordering Grand Canyon National Park. As he did at Steens Mountain, Babbitt vowed from the beginning that local people and their elected officials would have a say in the matter, but made it clear that he would be willing to push for national monument status if no consensus emerged.

Since then, he's attended two town hall meetings, in Flagstaff and Colorado City, Arizona, and has sought the support of area ranchers and government officials. Although he's emphasized that grazing and hunting will continue, local response to the plan remains largely negative.

"If Babbitt wanted to keep it pristine, then the best thing would be just to leave it alone," says Mohave County Supervisor Jim Zaborsky.

IF BABBITT WANTED TO KEEP IT PRISTINE, THEN THE BEST THING WOULD BE JUST TO LEAVE IT ALONE.

In August, two members of Arizona's congressional delegation responded to Babbitt's proposal with bills designed to head off a monument designation. Sen. Jon Kyl and Rep. Bob Stump, both Republicans, introduced separate bills that would create a Shivwits Plateau National Conservation Area. Stump's bill could bring paved roads into the area and requires a comprehensive mineral survey within two years. The proposal has the support of the Arizona Strip Regional Planning Task Force, a group of local officials from three counties in Utah and two in Arizona, the Kaibab Indian Reservation, and a variety of other interest groups. Mohave County Supervisor Carol Anderson, who chairs the task force, says Stump's proposal goes a long way toward soothing the worries of locals.

"We're all real concerned about the monument designation because of the effect it could have on the historical and cultural uses of the area," says Anderson. "The area is not at all prepared to handle an influx (of tourists)." She points out that the only access to the plateau is via 60 miles of dirt roads.

But in a congressional hearing in October, Babbitt slammed Stump's bill. "Several features of this legislation actually weaken protections in existing law," Babbitt said in his testimony.

Tom Robinson of the Grand Canyon Trust, a Flagstaff-based conservation group that is proposing a monument twice the size of Babbitt's proposal, calls the bill "not even fixable."

Sen. Kyl's bill is more compatible with Babbitt's vision, but it has attracted little attention and made almost no progress.

Locals remain suspicious of Babbitt's motives, and resent the attention their empty corner of the Southwest is suddenly receiving. Roger Taylor, the BLM field manager for the Arizona Strip, says that many in the area are "wondering why this is necessary." Taylor acknowledges that public interest and visitation to the Arizona Strip have increased slightly, but believes it's just a result of the rapid growth of nearby Las Vegas and St. George, Utah.

Robinson admits locals don't like all the talk of creating a new monument in their backyard. "I think they want this whole thing to go away," he says. "It's a tough call. It really is. I think there will be some short-term sacrifices—but in the long term there will be protection."

November 22, 1999

ONE PROPOSAL NEARLY RUNS AGROUND

by Ron Selden

⚜

LAST SPRING, INTERIOR SECRETARY Bruce Babbitt got to have some fun. He took a raft trip on Montana's Missouri River Breaks accompanied by author and filmmaker Dayton Duncan and historian Stephen Ambrose, author of *Undaunted Courage*, a recent and highly popular telling of the Lewis and Clark saga.

They floated past irrigated bottomlands and sage-dotted slopes, broad floodplains interspersed with high canyon walls, and eerie sandstone sculpted by water and wind. They may have sighted some of the deer and pronghorn antelope that feed in the croplands, and they may have spotted one of the bighorn sheep that perch on canyon overlooks.

Shortly after the trip, Babbitt said he was considering an unusual "segregation" order for part of the river and about 90,000 surrounding BLM-owned acres along the existing Wild and Scenic river corridor east of Great Falls. The temporary order was needed, he said, to freeze development in the area, especially new mining activity, and to help managers prepare for an expected onslaught of visitors during the bicentennial of the Lewis and Clark expedition.

Babbitt's plan was met with wails of protest from area landowners and some local government officials. Many are still bitter over the 1976 designation of a 149-mile Wild and Scenic river corridor on the Missouri, and they argued that the federal government exerts enough control on the river and its adjacent lands. Opponents also feared the order was a first step toward a new national monument or national park along the river.

Faced with growing opposition, Babbitt changed tack in July and withdrew the proposal. While he hasn't dismissed the idea of a national monument, he has distanced himself from talk of creating a new national park in the area, an action backed by Duncan and Ambrose, among others.

Now, he's pushing for the creation of a new and expanded National Conservation Area along the banks of the Missouri, where, he says, existing land uses such as grazing and farming can coexist with recreation. He promises the federal government will be a good neighbor to those whose families have toiled on their land for the past few generations.

"My principal concern... (is) to provide more protection to the on-the-ground resources," Babbitt said in October. "We can do this while celebrating and continuing uses that are compatible with the protection objectives."

While details are not yet fleshed out, Babbitt has asked the Central Montana Resource Advisory Council, which provides guidance to the Bureau of Land Management, to hold public hearings and come up with guidelines by the end of the year. He's asked the 15-member panel to develop proposals for managing the expected swarms of Lewis and Clark buffs. Also in the works is a potential permit system for river users, which would be a first for Missouri River floaters.

The controversy seems to have died down for now, and the committee is working overtime to meet Babbitt's year-end deadline. "Overall, I think the process is working," says Great Falls conservationist Jim McDermand, who serves on the committee. "I think most everyone wants to keep (the river) as it is and protect it from the hordes of tourists who are coming."

November 22, 1999

THE KING HAS COME
TO CLAIM MORE LAND

by Rochelle Oxarango

A WEEK AGO, one of our sheepherders told us a strange tale. It seems a helicopter had hovered over him and his herd early that morning. Not knowing anyone besides the government who could afford such luxuries, I had to assume that King William had sent his Knight in Flying Armor, Secretary of Interior Bruce Babbitt, on another crusade to claim a chunk of the West.

Only the day before, my husband and I had read about Babbitt's intentions to "protect" the Great Rift by adding it to the nearby Craters of the Moon National Monument in Idaho.

Such land grabs have occurred with increasing regularity during Bill Clinton's reign. Wielding the powerful scepter of the Antiquities Act of 1906, he has designated 3.1 million acres of new national monuments in Western states, more than any other president. But are these royal grabs necessary? And more importantly, are they right?

The Great Rift is an area of over 600 square miles best known for its relatively young lava beds. Currently, the 83-square-mile Craters of the Moon is the only part of the Great Rift designated as a national monument, managed by the

National Park Service. The rest is under the authority of the Bureau of Land Management.

Grazing is the main economic utility of this desert, and ranchers like us are very familiar with its landscape. The way to get the full effect of the desert is not by gliding overhead in a chopper, but by bouncing over the winding, dusty, muddy, lava rock roads at 2 mph. The conditions are so tough that the only people we see in our grazing area are fellow ranchers, a few hunters, and the occasional lost traveler.

> THE WAY TO GET THE FULL EFFECT OF THE DESERT IS NOT BY GLIDING OVERHEAD IN A CHOPPER, BUT BY BOUNCING OVER THE WINDING, DUSTY, MUDDY, LAVA ROCK ROADS AT 2 MPH.

The road situation works for us. We don't worry about the animals or herders getting hit by cars, and we generally don't have a problem with theft. For most people, the harsh wind, painful roads, abundance of rattlesnakes, inclement weather, and the high probability of getting lost are enough to keep them from wanting to recreate here. The Great Rift is a beautiful and unique environment, but it is unforgiving.

Babbitt would like to see higher federal protection. Our question is, protection from what? I can guarantee you that no development will be occurring in this area in the near future, if ever. For one, the land is already under the authority of the federal government. Two, the harsh climate makes it unappealing to developers. Three, farmers can't plow under the desert because of the lava rock. And four, industries will not find the Great Rift's lack of reasonable access and water very attractive.

So why are Clinton and Babbitt moving ahead anyway? According to an Associated Press article, the Clinton administration is trying to protect unique places from urban sprawl or oil and gas drilling. But there is not one oil well in the state of Idaho, and urban sprawl could only occur if a mass influx of people could convince the BLM to sell or exchange land.

Babbitt has tried to reassure ranchers that grazing would continue under the administration of BLM management in the expanded monument. Forgive me, but I'm not confident in the duration of that arrangement, for Babbitt also stated on our local news that he would like to see this area gain National Park status. Historically, hunting and grazing have been phased out of national parks.

BABBITT WOULD LIKE TO SEE HIGHER FEDERAL PROTECTION. OUR QUESTION IS, PROTECTION FROM WHAT?

Underneath all the rhetoric about locals and protecting America's natural legacy is the reality that King William and Sir Babbitt are trying to secure there own political legacies. In Clinton's case he may be trying to erase his royal screw-ups.

Instead, he has drawn attention to the Antiquities Act of 1906 and the need to change it. It's clear to many westerners that any attempts to create new national monuments should require Congressional approval.

Though the prospects are dim, I hope Clinton and Babbitt

back off on expanding Craters of the Moon National Monument. If they don't, I hope a new administration will reconsider
this designation and others like them in the West. Protecting
land that doesn't need protection is a foolish exercise that does
nothing for the land, while damaging the relationship between
the federal government and the local people who know the land.

If locals are concerned for the preservation of the Great Rift,
they will initiate the protection. Until that time, the royal helicopter
should be grounded.

BUSH CAMP BACKPEDALS ON TOPPLING MONUMENTS

by Tony Davis

VICE PRESIDENTIAL CANDIDATE Richard Cheney may have spoken too soon in August, when he said George W. Bush might rescind national monuments created by President Clinton. Cheney had earlier criticized Clinton for creating monuments "willy-nilly all over the West."

U.S. presidents have created 114 monuments under the 1906 Antiquities Act, and undoing them is unlikely, according to University of Colorado law professor Charles Wilkinson. In 1996, Wilkinson helped Interior Department Solicitor John Leshy draft Clinton's proclamation creating the Grand Staircase-Escalante National Monument in Utah.

Wilkinson cites a 1938 opinion by Attorney General Homer Cummings, who worked for Democratic President Franklin D. Roosevelt. The Interior secretary had asked Roosevelt to abolish the Castle Pinckney National Monument in Charleston, South Carolina, but Cummings concluded that the Antiquities Act didn't allow it.

"The Supreme Court hasn't spoken to that directly, but courts have given deference to attorney general opinions," says Wilkinson.

Harrison Dunning, a University of California-Davis law professor, sees things differently. "Cummings's opinion doesn't bind the courts," he says, "and I'd assume that since the president does it in the first place, another president can say 'I don't want it anymore.'"

Nonetheless, Cheney has backpedaled. While the Bush camp hasn't ruled out the possibility completely, Cheney press secretary Juleanna Glover Weiss repeats a statement about monuments that Bush made last June: "It is a very hard egg to unscramble."

September 25, 2000

MONUMENTAL CHANGES

by Matt Jenkins and Michelle Nijhuis

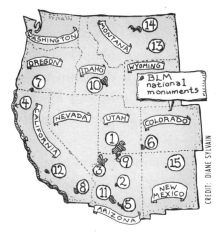

CREDIT: DIANE SYLVAIN

WITH ONLY THREE DAYS LEFT before George W. Bush would become president, the Clinton administration pressed forward with its land-protection plans and created seven new national monuments, six of them in the West.

- The Sonoran Desert National Monument in Arizona is the largest of the pack, encompassing over 486,000 acres of desert northeast of Organ Pipe National Monument. The area will be managed by the Bureau of Land Management, but about 84,000 acres are now within the U.S. Air Force's Goldwater Bombing Range; overflights will be allowed to continue.

- The 377,346-acre Upper Missouri River Breaks National Monument in central Montana includes part of the Lewis and Clark trail and one of the last free-flowing stretches of the Missouri.

- Carrizo Plain National Monument in central California, 204,107 acres, is a diverse grassland traversed by the San Andreas Fault.
- Kasha-Katuwe Tent Rocks National Monument in north-eastern New Mexico, 4,114 acres, is intended to protect an unusual group of large, tent-shaped volcanic rock formations.
- Pompeys Pillar National Monument in Montana, 51 acres, is a sandstone butte on the south side of the Yellowstone River. The rock was signed by William Clark of the Lewis and Clark expedition.
- Minidoka Internment National Monument in southern Idaho. The Idaho site, to be managed by the National Park Service, will commemorate the Japanese-Americans who were confined there by the U.S. government during World War II.

These monuments join 10 other BLM-managed monuments designated by President Clinton during his two terms:

- Grand Staircase-Escalante National Monument, Utah, 1,870,800 acres, designated September 1996.
- Agua Fria National Monument, Arizona, 71,100 acres, designated January 2000.
- Grand Canyon-Parashant National Monument, Arizona, 1,054,264 acres (managed jointly by the Park Service and the BLM), designated January 2000.
- California Coastal National Monument, California, 840 miles of coastline, designated January 2000.
- Ironwood Forest National Monument, Arizona, 129,022 acres, designated June 2000

- Canyons of the Ancients National Monument, Colorado, 163,852 acres, designated June 2000.
- Cascade-Siskyou National Monument, Oregon, 52,947 acres, designated June 2000.
- Santa Rosa and San Jacinto Mountains National Monument, California, 272,000 acres (managed jointly by the Forest Service and the BLM), designated October 2000.
- Vermilion Cliffs National Monument, Arizona, 279,550 acres, designated November 2000.
- Craters of the Moon National Monument, Idaho, 661,287 acres (managed jointly by the Park Service and the BLM), designated November 2000.

All 15 of the Bureau of Land Management monuments are part of the National Landscape Conservation System (NLCS), created by the BLM administration during Clinton's second term. The NLCS also included some 800 National Conservation Areas, wilderness areas and other protected areas that the BLM has managed for as long as 30 years. The new system is intended to give these lands some collective visibility—and a better shot at adequate funding from Congress. There might be a downside to that visibility, says a former agency staffer: "It just makes them easier to lop off."

January 29, 2001

BEYOND THE REVOLUTION

by Ed Marston

THE STRUGGLE FOR THE PUBLIC LANDS is ending. Now what happens? Will the Interior West remain a rogue region, or will it choose to rejoin America?

In the wake of the stunning 1994 victory by Newt Gingrich and his allies, Secretary of Interior Bruce Babbitt shuttled endlessly between Washington, D.C. and Denver, and then spent hours sitting at various negotiating roundtables, watching paint not just dry but blister and peel as ranchers and environmentalists attempted to settle their quarrel over the West's public lands.

Although he was criticized for wasting his time at these sessions, Denver was probably a better place for him to wait out the siege of the nation's capitol than the Interior building.

Now the waiting is over, and Bruce Babbitt is once again shuttling between Washington, D.C. and the Western United States. This time he is no passive observer of someone else's process. This time he comes West bearing a big stick and a small carrot. The stick is the Antiquities Act of 1906, and a threat to use it in a dozen or more places in the West to create national monuments, as President Bill Clinton did at Grand Staircase-

Escalante in Utah, and more recently in Arizona and California. The carrot is a promise not to create another national monument if local interests and their congressional representatives come up with and pass a bill to protect the land.

To add insult to the multiple injuries Babbitt is visiting on the West, Clinton, acting through Forest Service Chief Mike Dombeck, a Babbitt protégé, has locked up an additional 90,000 square miles of roadless land while the Forest Service studies ways to keep it roadless.

How has the Interior West reacted to these massive affronts? Various cowboy-hatted Paul Reveres are riding about raising the alarm. Shovels are being collected in significant numbers.

THIS TIME [BABBITT] COMES WEST BEARING A BIG STICK AND A SMALL CARROT.

Otherwise, the war between extractive interests and the environmental movement for control of the Interior West's public lands is drawing to a close. The timber era, the cattle era, the mainstem big-dam era, the wise-use era are ending. An immense landscape is going from one set of uses to another set of uses, from one way of life to another, in an astoundingly short time.

The transformation is occurring so quickly, and in so many places, that the conquered lands have not yet been occupied. Only Babbitt seems to understand what has happened, and so he has traveled ceaselessly from place to place, claiming 50,000 acres here, 150,000 acres there.

It is one thing to make these claims from Washington, D.C., as Clinton and Dombeck did with the roadless forest lands, or even as Babbitt does by coming to the West, to personally plant flags on the conquered lands. But the difficult task of administering these lands in new ways is being left to underfunded and demoralized federal agencies, struggling, amid often hostile communities, to understand what their new world looks like.

THE WAR BETWEEN EXTRACTIVE INTERESTS AND THE ENVIRONMENTAL MOVEMENT FOR CONTROL OF THE INTERIOR WEST'S PUBLIC LANDS IS DRAWING TO A CLOSE.

Dombeck, for example, takes command of 90,000 square miles, but he does it from the top, without the understanding or cooperation of his agency, most of whose employees wish they had never heard the word "roadless."

The agency with the best chance to make the changes is the Army Corps of Engineers, which is ponderously moving toward the destruction of dams it built only a few decades ago. When the first dam on the Snake River is breached, it will be clear to even the die-hards that one era has ended and another has begun.

How was an always touchy, seemingly sovereign region transformed? Why is the West sitting passively while this enormous change is wrought? The short answer is that the economy and the environmentalists, not necessarily in that order, have reworked the region. The West's myths and politics and power rest on control of the grass, gold, trees, and rushing water of the public lands, and that control is just about over.

The environmental movement fought the extractive

industry's control of the public lands on the ground, through endless appeals and lawsuits that challenged everything from the construction of billion-dollar dams to trivial changes in grazing permits for individual ranchers. Just as significantly, it fought nationally. The Sierra Club, the Wilderness Society, the National Audubon Society, and even the Nature Conservancy went over the heads of Western land users and elected officials to the 225 million Americans who do not live in the Interior West.

Over decades, working through thousands of magazine and newspaper articles and books and millions of pieces of direct mail, urban and suburban Americans were made aware that they owned immense tracts of land in the West.

The land, environmental groups told them, was simultaneously pristine and trashed. It was virgin and whore. It was the hope of America—a vast Statue of Liberty holding out its arms to the cramped masses in the cities and suburbs—and it was a helpless heroine lashed to the tracks of heedless Western development.

Those decades of work have paid off in the courts, in the arenas that hear appeals of federal actions, and even in attracting new breeds to the public-land management offices. But the work bore its most spectacular fruit in the midst of the Gingrich Revolution, when enough Midwestern and Eastern Republicans joined the Democrats in the U.S. House to prevent the rollback of laws like the Endangered Species Act and to stop the authorization of additional damage to the region's rivers and forests and grasslands. That political coalition defeated what may have been the West's final bid to continue to run the public lands as if they belonged only to the region.

It is one thing to achieve a victory with the help of an

aroused national constituency. It is another to govern the land day in and day out. And here, Clinton-Babbitt—or is it Babbitt-Clinton?—are severely handicapped. The national public pays only sporadic attention to the West's public lands—when wolves are reintroduced, when Yellowstone is diminished by air pollution from snowmobiles, when buffalo are slaughtered.

> IT IS ONE THING TO ACHIEVE A VICTORY WITH THE HELP OF AN AROUSED NATIONAL CONSTITUENCY. IT IS ANOTHER TO GOVERN THE LAND DAY IN AND DAY OUT.

But those who live near the public lands pay them full-time attention. And even with the flood of newcomers who have moved to the West—people who have still not figured out what is at stake in their new homeland—that attention is implacably hostile to the goals of this Democratic administration. The hostility is backed by a bloc of Western senators—men from Utah, Alaska, Wyoming, Montana, Arizona, New Mexico, Colorado, Idaho—who have negative agendas—blocking the administration on many fronts.

Most important, these senators are starving the land-management agencies, turning personnel into people of paperwork who rarely get to visit the land, let alone control it.

But those are the agendas they can no longer move. They have been reduced to obstructionism. And even here they fail now and again. They couldn't keep the wolves out. Babbitt every now and then gets to whack a small dam. And the move to dismantle the four Snake River dams has gotten further than most of us would have dreamed possible even two years ago.

By comparison with its senators, the West's governors have no power at all. State lands are tiny compared to federal lands, and state budgets are even smaller. If the governors are to have any influence, they must be united and they must fight in the arena of ideas and public policy. When it comes to the public lands and the environment, broad policies are set by the federal government. But these broad policies are then to be handed over to the states and local government for implementation.

The senators and governors each have their constituencies. The senators are backed by the logging and mining and oil and gas industries. The front guys of this movement are the wise-users, the sagebrush rebels, rural county governments, and the off-road vehicle users, who are well organized and who literally control the land.

But the governors also have a constituency. It is a patchwork quilt of watershed, consensus, collaboration, community-forestry, and range-restoration efforts that have appeared everywhere in the West, as if by magic, starting a decade ago.

We are in the midst of endless conflict because the West's debate over public lands and natural resources is dominated by the principle of sovereignty. A significant part of the environmental movement believes that the public lands can be protected only if the region is denied sovereignty. Meanwhile, those who most loudly proclaim the need for the West to be sovereign usually act as if freedom will vanish if the ability to drive motorized vehicles anywhere, or to shoot a firearm anywhere, or to graze a cow anywhere is abridged.

Behind this noise lie strong arguments for some local influence over the federal lands. Everything here—municipal reservoirs, sewage treatment, forest fires, a lost hiker, garbage disposal, and certainly economies—is a federal concern, because all involve the land-management agencies, the federal courts, the Congress, and the White House. While federal environmental laws affect the entire nation, the situation is more challenging in the West, where 50 percent of the land is also in federal hands.

WE ARE IN THE MIDST OF ENDLESS CONFLICT BECAUSE THE WEST'S DEBATE OVER PUBLIC LANDS AND NATURAL RESOURCES IS DOMINATED BY THE PRINCIPLE OF SOVEREIGNTY.

It is not enough to simply say: "These are public lands and they must be run by federal mandate." There must be more.

Not only the West has a stake in these new arrangements and relationships. The nation is also vitally concerned. So long as this remains a rogue region, fixated on the wrongs it is suffering, we cannot become an influential adult in the eyes of the rest of the country. We will always be intent on causing trouble, and on making alliances with other troublemakers.

It is not right that a region whose landscape and wildlife and rivers symbolize America to the rest of the world should simultaneously be its most alienated region. That must be changed.

April 10, 2000

✍

THE CHANGING OF THE GUARD

Stevens Arch in Escalante Canyon

INTERIOR VIEW IV

by Ed Marston

✍

MARSTON: Is there a chance that these national monuments will turn out to be meaningless gestures, that Congress in the next administrations could just ignore them, and they'll die?

BABBITT: It depends upon the public. Now, we hear a lot of big chest-thumping talk from members of Congress (about overturning them). If history is any guide, it won't be done. The monuments established by presidents—Republicans and Democrats over the 100 years—thrived; all of them. I think that public support will translate into an adequate level of attention. And, mark my words, the people who are out there opposing these monuments, 10 years from now will be saying that it was their idea; they'll be claiming credit for it. That's what history tells us. I don't think it's going to be any different in this case.

MARSTON: So when Gale Norton moves into your office, will she be able to get right to work on her approaches?

BABBITT: There is no question that we have changed the regulatory direction of the department in mining, grazing, and timber policy, and for that matter in energy extraction as well. And they may have a different agenda. But they will have to use the same process we used—that is, go through a long and public process of NEPA (National Environmental Policy Act) compliance, of procedural compliance with the environmental statutes. And that will give the public a look at the proposed changes and the chance to measure them and respond. That's the reason that I'm really quite confident that the important changes will endure: Because they have public support.

February 12, 2001

MONUMENTS CAUGHT
IN THE CROSSHAIRS

by Kirsten Bovee

⚘

WHEN GEORGE BUSH and Dick Cheney stumped for the presidency, they vowed to increase oil and gas exploration on public lands and to roll back newly designated monuments.

Environmentalists cringed.

But in the administration's early days, it seemed that campaign rhetoric might prove an empty promise, as lawmakers were reluctant to jump on the Bush bandwagon. When last December Rep. James Hansen, R-Utah, offered his support as head of the House Resources Committee to "deal with these millions of acres of new designations which circumvented the public process and the legislative process," there weren't many takers.

Rep. Tom Udall, D-N.M., declined Hansen's offer of assistance, saying that Clinton did nothing untoward in his designation of Tent Rocks National Monument in New Mexico. Udall says that in his district, "(former) Secretary Babbitt worked with the congressional delegation, pueblos, and the public to build consensus," and that Hansen was "just throwing red meat to his constituents."

But now the conservative rhetoric is coalescing into strategy as Western Republicans wage war on multiple fronts. Defenders of Clinton's 19 new monuments are bracing for a long four years.

STRATEGIES EMERGE

Already one piece of legislation that would affect an existing monument seems destined for congressional vote. The House Resources Committee has endorsed a bill by Rep. Mike Simpson, R-Idaho that would reintroduce hunting in the expanded portions of Craters of the Moon National Monument in his home state. Because it appears that the Clinton administration never intended to ban hunting, a prior use of the land, environmentalists have not put up a fight.

Western Republicans are also trying to amend the process by which national monuments are created. Simpson is drafting a National Monument Fairness Act to mandate greater congressional and state involvement in the designation of monuments larger than 50,000 acres. "We're not trying to undermine the Antiquities Act," he says, "but Congress needs to be involved in these decisions."

Interior Secretary Gale Norton echoed and amplified Hansen's and Simpson's efforts with letters to state officials that asked, "Are there boundary adjustments that the department should be considering? Are there existing uses inside these monuments that we should accommodate?"

Environmentalists worry that the Bush administration could bypass the legislative process altogether to undo some of the land protections currently afforded by national monument status. Though Norton has said her intervention will stop short of repealing Clinton's monuments, Melanie Griffin, public-lands director of the Sierra Club, says, "You don't have to undesignate a monument to destroy it."

Monument defenders say the administration is manipulating fears of an impending energy crisis to garner support for changes in land protections. Vice President Cheney and Interior officials are drafting an energy plan that looks to remove drilling and exploration restrictions on protected federal lands. In a separate U.S. Geological Survey report commissioned by the House Resources Committee, six Western monuments designated by the Clinton administration, including Grand Staircase-Escalante and Canyons of the Ancients, were listed as containing a "moderate to high probability" of coal, gas or oil reserves.

"They're using the energy issues as an excuse to open public lands to exploitation and decrease environmental protection," says Faith Weiss of the Natural Resources Defense Council.

Clinton's presidential proclamations establishing the new monuments withdraw the lands from any new mineral, gas, or oil leasing. But the Bush administration has staked out the legal position that the president retains the authority to revise these protections. In a motion to dismiss a case that calls for a repeal of six of Clinton's monuments, brought last year by the Mountain States Legal Foundation, the Bush administration maintains that the president holds the right to both designate and modify national monuments.

If Bush or Norton act to shrink the monuments or alter management plans to allow for drilling, the courts may be called upon to clarify whether such actions are legal. Jim Angell of Earthjustice Legal Defense Fund says there has never been any lawsuit brought over changes to national monuments.

"There's very little law on this issue," he says. "The new argument is emerging that basically the president can do whatever he wants."

April 23, 2001

Monument Status
Could Wreck Ruins

by Gail Binkly

THE ARCHAEOLOGICAL RUINS of the Southwest have long posed a thorny management problem. People love to see them; the tourism industry wants to promote them. But the more these fragile remnants of ancient cultures are visited, the more damage they suffer.

Walking the tightrope between preservation and promotion is nowhere more of a challenge than at Canyons of the Ancients, the newly designated national monument west of Cortez, Colorado.

"We have to be really careful," says LouAnn Jacobson, the monument's manager and a Bureau of Land Management employee for 21 years. "We're already getting more inquiries, people coming in with specific names of places they want to go." In many cases, the backcountry ruins they name aren't developed or protected, and officials can only "try to give sort of a gentle message that they aren't ready for a lot of visitors."

The 164,000-acre monument contains, by conservative estimate, 20,000 archaeological sites, ranging from scattered potsherds to standing structures. Most have not been surveyed, excavated, or stabilized, and for decades their main protection was their obscurity. But since Clinton's designation of the monument on June 9, 2000, Canyons of the Ancients has drawn increasing attention from both the public and such popular publications as *National Geographic* and *Modern Maturity*.

Additional funding will be critical if monument officials are to handle the impacts of increased tourism, says Jacobson, who has asked for a budget of around $1 million for fiscal year 2002. How much of that will be granted is uncertain. New Interior Secretary Gale Norton has said there is no money to carry out plans for all the new monuments Clinton designated during his last year in office. And, Jacobson admits, "It's always an uphill battle for BLM to get additional funding for anything."

But she is optimistic that Congress will provide additional money for ruins stabilization and repair, more staff, and archaeological inventories. The monument is already hiring a new law-enforcement officer to help the lone BLM ranger who now patrols more than 800,000 acres in southwest Colorado.

At local meetings before Clinton's proclamation, Mark Varien of the Crow Canyon Archaeological Center in Cortez raised concerns about calling attention to the area. "I said the worst-case scenario would be to designate a monument and then not get the funding appropriated," he says, "because designating a monument is going to create increased impacts."

MANAGING STYLES DIFFER

The ancestral Native Americans who inhabited the Four Corners area prior to 1300 A.D. left countless relics, from stone tools and yucca sandals to petroglyphs and crumbling structures. Pothunters and vandals have taken their toll on these artifacts, but well-meaning "site-seers" also cause problems.

Backcountry ruins have seen a dramatic increase in visitation over the last 20 years, "and the accompanying impacts to the resources have been observable," Varien says.

Public-lands officials manage ruins in different ways. Ten miles east of the new monument, at Mesa Verde National Park, protection is paramount. The backcountry is closed; tourists view most of the park's spectacular ancestral Puebloan sites from a distance or while on guided tours.

But few land managers have the resources or the inclination to safeguard archaeological sites in such a manner. Instead, they try to funnel visitors to more developed ruins and minimize recreation at lesser-known sites.

Officials at the Southeast Utah group of national parks and monuments, which includes Canyonlands, Arches, Hovenweep, and Natural Bridges, have developed a cultural-site information policy, explains Paul Henderson, the group's chief of interpretation and visitor services.

Ruins are categorized on a four-point scale. Class 1 contains sites that are widely known, Henderson says: "We readily disclose them to the public; they have a long history of tourist use." Class 4 sites are so fragile they're officially closed to visitation. "We withhold information about them from the public, and even from park staff. If people find them on their own, that's fine," Henderson says. Only Class 1 and Class 2 sites are depicted in park brochures and trail guides, he says.

Envisioning an Outdoor Museum

At Canyons of the Ancients, Jacobson hopes to follow the strategy of drawing visitors to a few major sites and leaving the rest, most of which are unimpressive rubble mounds, to the adventurous to find.

The BLM has not yet written a long-term management plan. First, Norton must give the go-ahead for an advisory committee that will assist with the effort, and then its members must be chosen. But Jacobson envisions the monument as an "outdoor museum" without the concessions and paved paths of Mesa Verde, but a place where people can "go explore, hopefully have respect for what they find, and have a sense of discovery, without just being led to places."

[MONUMENTS SHOULD BE] A PLACE WHERE PEOPLE CAN GO EXPLORE, HOPEFULLY HAVE RESPECT FOR WHAT THEY FIND, AND HAVE A SENSE OF DISCOVERY, WITHOUT JUST BEING LED TO PLACES.

"There's a hope that increased visibility may ultimately get us the resources we need to do a better job," she adds. "I view Canyons of the Ancients as a place where, if you have the resources, it doesn't have to be locked up to protect it."

Kristie Arrington, a Durango-based archaeologist who has

been with the BLM more than 20 years, agrees education can be an effective management tool. She recalls how Sand Canyon, a popular hiking area within the monument, suffered damage as it became widely known. Visitation jumped 2,000 percent from 1986 to 1996. Careless hikers knocked stones from ruin walls, trails proliferated, graffiti appeared on ancient structures, and artifacts disappeared. "That was very disheartening," she says.

Land managers decided to push a "leave-no-trace" message rather than heavy-handed restrictions. Since then, Arrington says, "I have seen the loss of resources dramatically decline."

Varien of the Crow Canyon Center concurs that education is the key, because law officers' capabilities are limited on the sprawling landscape. "It's just too big," he says.

An ancestral Puebloan tower featured (but not named) in the Canyons of the Ancients poster and logo has already drawn interest, and Jacobson admits it will probably have to have a minimal parking area before long.

"One of the ways we were trying to reduce the numbers (of visitors) was to kind of keep the area low-profile," Arrington says. "Obviously, that's not an option any more."

April 23, 2001

ENERGY PLAN EYES THE ROCKIES

by Michelle Nijhuis

GLORIA FLORA HAD BEEN HAVING a good month. On May 7, a federal judge upheld the former forest supervisor's 1997 decision to ban oil and gas development on parts of Montana's Rocky Mountain Front. A few days later, Flora traveled from her home in Helena, Montana, to Redfish Lake in Idaho, where she spoke to an appreciative crowd from the Idaho Conservation League.

On May 17, President Bush's energy policy hit the streets.

"I knew what was coming, so it wasn't like my mouth was hanging open or anything," says Flora, who left the Forest Service in 1999. "But I found it sad, and odd. It's as though the leader of the free world has put the vehicle in reverse. He's taking us back to the past."

For Flora, the saddest part of the 168-page report was an oblique reference to her decision on the Rocky Mountain Front. As supervisor of the Lewis and Clark National Forest in central Montana, she had placed a 10-to-15 year ban on oil and gas drilling in her forest's section of an energy-rich geological area. Her decision was a victory for environmentalists, tribes, and

many local residents, all of whom had pushed for years to protect the Front's jagged granite peaks and diverse wildlife.

The report from the president's energy policy team says that
many such protections are "appropriate," but it recommends that
the secretary of Interior "review and modify—restrictions where opportunities exist."

THE [BUSH ENERGY] POLICY HINTS THAT FOREST SUPERVISORS AND MONUMENT MANAGERS CAN EXPECT NOT ONLY MORE DRILLING ON AND NEAR THE PUBLIC LANDS, BUT ALSO MORE PIPELINES, POWER PLANTS, AND ELECTRIC TRANSMISSION LINES.

The policy hints that forest supervisors and monument managers can expect not only more drilling on and near the public lands, but also more pipelines, power plants, and electric transmission lines. With many of the top spots in the Department of Interior still open, agency staffers at all levels are scrambling to figure out the fine points. "We haven't heard anything," says Bonnie Dearing of the Lewis and Clark National Forest. "Not a single word."

"We're always hearing rumors, but we don't know what they mean," adds Gary Slagel, the interim superintendent of the Upper Missouri River Breaks National Monument in eastern Montana. "We're not getting the information we need."

The Lean is On

The details of the energy policy may be foggy, but it's clearly focused on coal, oil, and natural gas. The Rocky Mountains are rich in natural gas, which is fast becoming the country's dominant source of electricity. So the report is quick to point out that 40 percent of the gas on federal lands in the Rockies is off-limits to exploration.

That sounds like a big number, but the details tell a different story. A recent report from the National Petroleum Council, an industry advisory group to the secretary of Energy, says that only nine percent of the gas-rich lands are closed to leasing or "surface occupancy" by drill rigs and other equipment. Another 32 percent of the lands are subject to seasonal and temporary closures, usually put in place to protect breeding wildlife.

These numbers don't include the new national monuments in the Rockies, two of which have some natural gas potential. Those monuments, the Canyons of the Ancients in southwestern Colorado and the Upper Missouri River Breaks, honor existing leases but are closed to new leasing.

Rolling back the year-round restrictions, including those in the new national monuments, wouldn't be easy. A reversal of the Rocky Mountain Front ban, for example, would require another environmental impact statement and years of painful politics. Though the Secretary of the Interior can influence management plans for the monuments, says Larry Finfer of the Bureau of Land Management, major boundary changes would require the approval of Congress.

Changes to seasonal and temporary closures would also require environmental review, but the partial restrictions may be more vulnerable than the high-profile drilling bans.

The day after the president released his new policy, he signed two executive orders. One requires agencies to consider the impacts of land-use restrictions on energy supply, distribution, and use; the other calls for agencies to "expedite" energy-related projects.

Flora says her former colleagues in the federal agencies may already be feeling the heat from the top. "There's probably a lot of subtle pressure to cooperate, framed in very polite words," she says. "I'm sure the lean is on."

The "lean" may also affect federal lands with few existing protections, such as the Red Desert in southern Wyoming. Even Mac Blewer of the Wyoming Outdoor Council describes the area as a "gold mine," and the Bureau of Land Management had long planned to increase energy development in the Red Desert's Jack Morrow Hills. But last November, a visit from then-Interior Secretary Bruce Babbitt promised to change those plans. Babbitt asked the Bureau of Land Management to come up with a new "preferred alternative" for its environmental impact statement, one that would favor wildlife and scenery over oil and gas drilling.

The administration's new direction "could throw that whole process out of kilter," says Blewer. "We could be in a lot of trouble."

THE FOUR P'S

For all the Bush administration's eagerness to grab for gas, the industry may not be ready to step up to the plate. Gas prices have shot up over the past three years, and industry officials say they're already maxed out. "There aren't enough rigs and people to get it out," says Ken Wonstolen of the Colorado Oil and Gas Association. Though he's pleased that the administration wants to review existing restrictions, he says, "I don't know if (the new policy) is going to have any dramatic effects at all."

Supply is only one of the bottlenecks in the region's energy network, says Wonstolen. "We talk about the four P's—producers, processors, pipes, and power generators," he says. "We have problems with all four of those."

Though the administration's promised increases in production have gotten most of the attention, other parts of the energy infrastructure are also giving environmentalists and land managers cause for concern. Dozens of gas-fired power plants are in the works in Washington, Nevada, California, Arizona, and other states, and the administration's policy promises to smooth out their regulatory paths.

Jon Shumaker, an archaeologist whose work helped establish the new Ironwood Forest National Monument in southern Arizona, is almost single-handedly fighting a $1 billion power plant planned for just outside the monument's boundaries. "The brown clouds over Phoenix and Tucson are merging," says Shumaker, "and this plant is going to finish the job."

THE BROWN CLOUDS OVER PHOENIX AND TUCSON ARE MERGING, AND THIS PLANT IS GOING TO FINISH THE JOB.

Arizona Gov. Jane Hull wants to make sure her state's new monuments don't stand in the way of the power-plant expansion. When Interior Secretary Gale Norton asked governors for their comments on the monuments, Hull asked for boundary changes that would open up access for transmission lines.

At the same time, many Western politicians are unhappy about a policy recommendation that would grant eminent-domain authority to the federal government for new transmission lines. The Western Governors' Association, worried about the possible condemnation of private property, has formed a task force on the issue. Republican Sen. Pete Domenici and Democratic Sen. Jeff Bingaman, both of New Mexico, and Republican Sen. Larry Craig of Idaho all have voiced strong opposition to the proposal.

With support from different segments of the political spectrum, says Gloria Flora, activists like Shumaker might ultimately have public opinion on their side. She hopes the administration will eventually have a series of hearings on its policy, not unlike the Forest Service's tour for its roadless rule. "I dare them to have 600 public meetings on this energy policy," she says. "They'd be fun. They'd be more than fun."

June 4, 2001

NO GAME PLAN FOR THE PUBLIC LANDS

by Rebecca Clarren

JAY WATSON THOUGHT THE BUSH administration had finally given him something to celebrate. On December 28, Mark Rey, U.S. Department of Agriculture undersecretary of natural resources, announced that he had approved the Sierra Nevada Framework, the U.S. Forest Service's ambitious and controversial management plan that calls for less logging and grazing on 11 public forests in California.

"We are thoroughly delighted," crowed Watson, the California-Nevada regional director of The Wilderness Society. "After a decade of work, the decision is a victory for conservation."

But the party didn't last long.

Four days later, Jim Blackwell, the regional forester who oversees the Sierra Range, announced that the Framework is still a work in progress. Based on a directive from Rey to make more locally based decisions, Blackwell will consider how the plan affects recreation and livestock grazing, and amend it to include more logging.

"This is a direct attack on the Framework," says Watson. "Certainly, Mark Rey knew when he made his announcement that four days later they would launch a full-scale review. This was a clearly choreographed set of events."

Surprisingly, greens aren't the only ones upset. Off-road vehicle users and loggers wanted Bush to gut the entire plan, and they say a review spells revision, not rejection. Now threats of lawsuits fly through the air like jabs in a boxing ring.

The heated and confusing scenario resembles many Bush administration reviews of Clinton-era regulations. On a national level, Interior Department officials are examining ways to weaken new provisions in both the Clean Air and Clean Water acts. In the Intermountain West, the administration is reviewing initiatives that would prohibit road-building in national forests, ban snowmobiles from national parks, and reintroduce grizzly bears in Montana and Idaho. Yet most pundits say revising Clinton-era policies is a far cry from a proactive Western public-lands agenda.

> MOST PUNDITS SAY REVISING CLINTON-ERA POLICIES IS A FAR CRY FROM A PROACTIVE WESTERN PUBLIC-LANDS AGENDA.

"There's clearly no overarching natural resource strategy," says John Freemuth, senior fellow with the Andrus Center for Public Policy in Boise, Idaho. "We're all waiting for more clear data points."

A PASSIVE PROTOCOL

There are three quick and easy explanations why the administration has yet to devise a game plan for public lands: a disputed election, an anemic economy, and September 11. But even administration supporters complain that Bush's attention to the West is relatively slight.

When Bruce Babbitt was confirmed as Clinton's Interior secretary in 1993, he immediately began to push an aggressive agenda to increase grazing fees on the public lands and impose mining regulations. In the third month of the Clinton administration, both the president and the vice president flew to Portland, Oregon, and met with loggers, conservationists, and scientists over the spotted owl fracas. By July of his first year in office, Clinton had announced the Northwest Forest Plan, an ecosystem management plan for 24 million acres of forests in Washington, Oregon, and northern California.

ONE YEAR INTO ITS TERM, SUB-CABINET LEVEL POSITIONS, THE REAL POLICY WORKER BEES OF THE INTERIOR, ARE STILL VACANT.

"The previous administration got involved with us right up front," says Chris West of the pro-timber American Forest Resource Council. "(The Bush administration) has said a lot of good things, but at this point it's hard to say what they'll do. The jury's still out."

There are other indications that the public lands aren't a high priority for this administration. One year into its term, sub-cabinet level positions, the real policy worker bees of the Interior, are still vacant.

"Right now, BLM appointments are just being considered," says Freemuth. "Clearly, if they had some major agenda, those (acting directors) would be long gone."

Still, some conservationists say that the public shouldn't assume this apparent lack of strategy is good for the environment. At a recent press conference held by the environmental law firm Earthjustice, executive director Vawter "Buck" Parker announced that due to a fear of bad press, the administration has allowed a broad range of these reviews to wind up in the courts.

"There is a disturbing pattern where industry sues to overturn environmental regulations and the Justice Department puts up only the feeblest of defenses and refuses to appeal adverse decisions," says Parker. "The courts have become the forum of choice for rolling back environmental protections."

The court case over the Clinton-era proposed ban on snowmobiles in Yellowstone National Park is a good example, says Parker. Last April, the administration announced its support for the rule and allowed it to go into effect. But when the snowmobile industry sued the government, the administration didn't defend the law. Instead, it entered into negotiations with the industry to settle the suit and devise a new plan.

Similarly, when a district court judge blocked the roadless rule, a Clinton-created policy that protects 58.5 million acres of federal forest from road building, the Justice Department missed the July deadline to appeal the ruling. Due to nine other ongoing lawsuits, the administration says, it is working to revise the rule.

This seeming passivity is actually a sophisticated strategy, says Parker, because it allows Bush to make major changes in policy without involving Congress, and the public can't trace who's responsible.

"The judicial process in our country depends on two parties making the strongest case (they) can," he says. "When the administration purposely makes a weak argument, it subverts the entire democratic process."

Environmentalists say that another pillar of democracy, the media, is also hamstrung.

"In light of September 11, the news hole of environmental news coverage has shrunk dramatically," says Bruce Hamilton, conservation director of the Sierra Club. "People don't have a clue what Bush is doing."

THE DRILL FOR 2002

While administration officials say the public should expect some new and exciting proposals in the coming year, they remain lean on specifics. Ask Undersecretary Rey what proactive policies his agency is developing and he gives one example: energy. In order to increase energy development on public lands and encourage innovative projects, he says, the Forest Service is looking into ways to streamline both the National Environmental Policy Act and the Endangered Species Act.

The Interior Department is also working on some new policies, says Lynn Scarlett, assistant secretary for policy, management, and budget. The Interior budget currently has $100 million dedicated to developing private-landowner incentive programs, such as encouraging landowners to remove invasive species on their property by providing technical assistance, tax credits, financial resources, or scientific advice. Other collaborative projects between environmentalists, landowners, and government are in the works, says Scarlett.

"The goal is to inspire private landowners to proactively participate in conservation efforts and put emphasis on cooperation and results," says Scarlett. "If we could leave at the end of four years and feel like the greater preponderance of decisions were made through collaboration, we'd be happy."

If the administration is smart, it will initiate these collaborative approaches before it implements its national energy plan, says Chris Wood, former assistant to Forest Service Chief Mike Dombeck. Otherwise, says Wood, the Bush administration will be ramming policy down the public's throat—something it has routinely accused the Clinton administration of doing.

"It gets down to the maturity of the administration to recognize that conservation of the public lands is inevitable," says Wood. "You can wish the clock back 20 years, but whether through lawsuits or elections or editorials, the public will turn against ill-advised development."

February 4, 2002

NEW MONUMENTS:
PLANNING BY NUMBERS

by Jon Margolis

ՀՋ

RETURN WITH US NOW to those thrilling days of yesteryear, just before and after George W. Bush was inaugurated, when some of his Western supporters spoke openly about nullifying those 11 new national monuments created by the presidential predecessor they hated.

Enter reality, both legal and political. It turns out that the law on un-creating monuments does not exist. And to the apparent surprise of some Western Republicans, it turned out that most folks—even most Westerners—thought they were a good idea.

So in one manner or another they are here to stay. But in what manner? The presidential proclamations leave many blanks, to be filled in by the Bureau of Land Management, in whose tender care the monuments were placed.

Until late April, that care resembled what an earlier administration once called benign neglect. As various interested parties waited, the BLM and its parent Interior Department did…well, nothing. A few quasi-official meetings were cancelled because there was nothing to discuss. The elaborate planning process required under the law could not begin until Department of Interior said "go." So nothing began.

No wonder, then, that on April 24, when Interior Secretary Gale Norton finally announced her intention "to develop plans managing the national monuments established under the Department's jurisdiction in 2000 and 2001" (that's government jargon for "Go"), the environmental fraternity expressed "cautious optimism." The optimism comes from relief that something is finally being done. The caution comes from a paucity of confidence in the folks who are doing the doing.

Nor was confidence in any way upgraded when Norton said she wanted to make "the planning process a model of how to involve the people who live and work closest to these monuments."

To those already distrustful of the Administration, that could sound rather like an intention to give the locals veto power over the final management plans. And since the locals tend to be dominated (or in some cases, intimidated) by commercial interests and/or political-psychological hostility to preservation, those final management plans could end up allowing more mining, drilling, grazing, and driving than the resources can tolerate.

FINAL MANAGEMENT PLANS COULD END UP ALLOWING MORE MINING, DRILLING, GRAZING, AND DRIVING THAN THE RESOURCES CAN TOLERATE.

The driving might be more of a problem than the drilling. Only one of the new monuments—the Canyons of the Ancients in southwestern Colorado—has extensive petroleum deposits. But most of them are regularly visited by all-terrain vehicle drivers, and in the case of the Cascade-Siskiyou Monument in Oregon, by recreational miners who bring their own bulldozers.

Adena Cook, the public-lands director for the Blue Ribbon Coalition, which champions the cause of mechanized recreators, says her organization "will be working to keep open" the roads and trails its members now use. The Coalition will not, however, seek rules allowing off-road vehicles to wander all over the monuments.

"Oh, heavens no," she says. "All use needs to be managed. All that needs to be evaluated on a site-specific basis."

None of this is likely to satisfy environmentalists convinced that even the existing level of zipping and zooming degrades the values for which the monuments were established. Nor are they likely to be comforted by Cook's insistence that the monument decision-making "has to be locally based."

This could depend on how one defines "local." In Montana, for instance, some of the neighboring ranchers, gas speculators, and motorized river-rafters appear unhappy about the new Missouri River Breaks National Monument northeast of Great Falls. But polls leave little doubt that most Montanans are all for it.

In fact, despite the conservationist chorus of complaints— that the public comment "scoping" periods are too short, that the public meetings might be held in remote areas hard for their supporters to reach, that the Administration pays them no mind —political and legal realities might still combine to provide the new monuments with ample protection.

The law does not give BLM complete discretion, and federal workers tend to take their jobs seriously. So, for instance, when the preliminary management statement for the Canyons of the Ancients Monument in Colorado holds that "the area will be managed...so as not to create any new impacts that would interfere with the proper care and management of the objects protected by the designation," it's reasonable to assume that the BLM's draft management plan will reflect that approach.

Of course, the professionals in the National Park Service called for banning snowmobiles in Yellowstone National Park, a judgment politicians in the Bush administration seem intent on sabotaging. But these politicians are practicing dumb politics, as some Republican strategists concede (though not for publication). The monument process that Gale Norton just began will take about two years, meaning that final decisions will come in mid-2004, months before the next Presidential election. Bush's approval rating remains high, but it is slipping. On no subject is he rated lower than on environmental policy.

So how is it in his interest to pick yet another fight with the conservation community, even over one of the esoteric environmental issues?

It isn't. Adena Cook says the Blue Ribbon Coalition speaks for some 600,000 Americans. Almost 50 million Americans visited a national monument last year. As the late, great, Richard J. Daley said, the first thing a politician has to learn to do is count.

May 13, 2002

ENERGY BOOM'S FORWARD GUARD STALLS OUT IN UTAH...FOR NOW

by Adam Burke

THUMPER TRUCKS HAVE been rolling over this rugged chunk of public land a few miles from Arches National Park for only a few days, but already they are causing concern. News articles in Western and national newspapers have drawn attention to the machines. More than once, stories have told of "thumper trucks, pounding the earth in a seismic search for oil deposits..."

Writer Terry Tempest Williams, an ardent defender of Utah's redrock desert, penned an essay for the *New York Times* that characterized the trucks as "giant mechanical insects."

"At the time, the Bush energy plan was at best an abstraction and at worst a secret," Tempest Williams said later. "I wanted to give the American public a picture of what was happening on the ground in Utah."

It's early February, and I'm heading south off Interstate 70, near Cisco, Utah, in search of the thumpers, which have, deservedly or not, become a symbol of the Bush energy policy in the Intermountain West. A helicopter passes over head, with a basket cabled to its belly: seismic gear moving from a central staging area to crews working somewhere on this 36-square-mile area.

Soon I see truck treads unfurl off the road alongside pink flagging and something like a long extension cord. The trucks have rolled over many things: soft, lumpy soil; rocks, bunch grasses, blackbrush, even a few juniper trees. But when I find them, they are temporarily stuck down in the nearest drainage. The lead driver makes several charges up a steep incline, giant tires chewing the embankment. The engine roar is deafening.

They finally make it out of the draw, and I get a closer look: They *are* segmented like insects; the center section, a tangle of hydraulic pipes and pistons, bears a steel plate the size of a card table. With a shudder and belch of exhaust, the trucks slowly drop their plates to the earth in unison. A low bass tone is barely audible above the engine noise. Tiny grains of sand and dust dance and skitter across the soil surface, like ants swarming out of the ground.

THE BACKLASH [THUMPER TRUCKS] PROVOKE AT DOME PLATEAU FORESHADOWS AN ESCALATING WAR OVER ENERGY DEVELOPMENT IN THE INTERMOUNTAIN WEST.

This scene is repeated hundreds of times over the next several days on Dome Plateau, while more headlines break across the national news about the Bush administration's push for more oil and gas development on public lands. A little research reveals that these trucks won't reduce Utah's signature sandstone arches to rubbled dust. But there's no denying that the backlash they provoke at Dome Plateau foreshadows an escalating war over energy development in the Intermountain West.

WHAT'S IN A NAME?

But first things first: The 40,000-pound trucks don't thump. They don't "pound the earth," as news stories continue to report, and are actually much more precise and gentle than old-school exploration. They have to be. The days of striking large fields of black gold by accident are long gone. Only smaller, unproven reserves remain on public lands.

Known in the industry as "vibroseis vehicles," the trucks move in a straight line across miles of terrain, stopping in 220-foot increments to send sound waves into the ground. The waves rebound off various geologic features below the earth's surface, and then are picked up by arrays of sensors or "geophones" inserted into the ground. The sound is conveyed via miles of cables and battery packs to a central recording bank. The result is a highly detailed picture that can show an area as large as 300 square miles, and thousands of feet deep.

INDUSTRY OFFICIALS SAY MODERN SEISMIC EXPLORATION ACTUALLY INCREASES ENVIRON-MENTAL PROTECTION.

Industry officials say modern seismic exploration actually increases environmental protection. These trucks, which have been in use for decades, allow oil and gas developers to drill with surgical precision, greatly reducing the number of exploratory wells. The balloon tires and articulated mid-section make cross-country travel easy and road building unnecessary.

"Most companies have equipped them with very large tires that spread out the weight so that in terms of actual pounds per square inch there's no more than an average vehicle," says Stuart

Wright, a geophysicist for Western GeCo, the energy contractor exploring at Dome Plateau. "It's our contention that any impact is minimal and ephemeral. It tends to heal itself rather quickly. But if you don't want to take our word for it, you can go out there and judge for yourself."

Such light-footed mobility has led industry and the Bureau of Land Management to view the thumper trucks as a relatively minor intrusion. On Dome Plateau, the agency's decision to permit Western GeCo to conduct seismic work concluded that the project would "not result in any undue and unnecessary environmental degradation."

But several other agencies raised concerns, especially about soil disturbance, which, in the desert, can lead quickly to wind and water erosion. Letters from the U.S. Geological Survey, the U.S. Fish and Wildlife Service, and the Environmental Protection Agency all said the BLM's draft environmental assessment was lacking.

Jayne Belnap, a soil scientist with USGS's Moab office, took issue with the BLM's suggestion that soil and vegetation would recover in three to five years. "Recovery of soil compaction, biological soil crusts, and most desert shrubs (in this desert system) is on the order of at least multiple decades," Belnap wrote.

These letters, in counterpoint to internal BLM memos, raised the hackles of the Southern Utah Wilderness Alliance (SUWA), which claimed that the BLM was favoring energy development at the expense of environmental protection and public input.

The group circulated an August 2001 memo from BLM's Utah office that instructs Utah field offices make drilling and leasing their "No. 1 priority."

But Maggie Wyatt, manager of the BLM's Moab Field Office, says she wasn't pressured to go ahead with the project. "These are lands that have been leased for over five years," says Wyatt. "It's not BLM policy that dictates whether a company decides to explore or drill. It's market prices."

Wyatt admits the trucks damage fragile soils, but says "the area of disturbance represents a very small part of the project area—less than one percent. So we found this to be an impact that was not significant."

SUWA and several other groups thought otherwise. They asked for a stay on the Dome Plateau project from the Interior Board of Land Appeals (IBLA), presenting photos of the trucks working in wet soils, and close-up shots of deep tire ruts.

On February 22, the IBLA shut down the one-week-old project, raising concerns that the BLM had not analyzed a full range of alternative actions, ignored the comments of sister agencies, and may have acted in an "arbitrary and capricious" manner. The BLM and the company said the delay would cost Western GeCo upwards of $40,000 a day while crews waited on stand-by, but the IBLA's director of appeals Robert More wrote: "A delay of four to seven months and the attendant costs pale by comparison to resource harms lasting decades or even centuries."

MAKING WAVES

The IBLA stay immediately raised the public scrutiny of seismic projects, and stepped up the level of caution within BLM. The Vernal, Utah, BLM field office has a seismic project under review, and though it won't involve vibroseis vehicles, citizens are already calling the field office to voice objections.

The agency is also reviewing a 19-square-mile thumper truck project for the Canyons of the Ancients National Monument in southwestern Colorado.

"We want to learn from the vulnerabilities that were identified with the (Dome Plateau) environmental assessment, and demonstrate to the public that we fully considered the range of the alternatives out here," says Helen Mary Johnson of the BLM's Durango field office, who recently released a draft environmental assessment of the canyons project for public comment.

All told, there are at least half a dozen seismic projects of various sizes proposed on BLM land in the next several months, adding to what activists say has been several years of acceleration of seismic exploration projects. In the Green River Basin of southwestern Wyoming, at least eight projects were carried out last fall alone, says Dan Heilig, executive director for the Wyoming Outdoor Council.

"That's more than the previous decade," he says, "and we're talking about big projects — 200, even 300 square miles."

Heilig says that while the increases in exploration and drilling may be driven by market forces, the pressure on BLM field offices from the top is leaving less and less time for discussion and analysis.

"What we're seeing are subtle shifts in the way permits are handled, and a limiting of public involvement whenever possible," says Heilig. "Thumper trucks aren't the worst (impact) we see, but they are a step in that process that leads to more development."

STALKING THE ELUSIVE ENERGY POLICY

For almost a year, the Bush administration has made clear in agency memos and promises to the American public that increasing energy development on public lands is a top priority. In March, the BLM came forward with an outline for how it plans to accomplish this goal. At a two-day summit in Denver, agency officials outlined a 43-part task list that includes efforts to speed up the permitting process for leases and drilling permits and to "streamline" environmental review. The agency is also revising land-use plans, which may alter various seasonal protections for wildlife, and open up new areas to exploration. And the BLM may reduce the royalties companies pay to drill on public land.

The plan received qualified praise from industry representatives. "This is a good first step, but it's very general," says Ken Leonard, senior manager for the American Petroleum Institute. "What we need now is for the BLM to move toward a permitting process that is not designed to delay but rather to decide."

Citizen and environmental groups in attendance were skeptical.

"BLM simply does not have the manpower to properly go out and do environmental assessments and studies on the effects of this drilling," said Jim Baca, who headed the BLM for two years during the Clinton administration. "They have about the same amount of people today as they did 10 years ago, their budgets have been continually cut, and so they don't really have the expertise in place to make good decisions."

The BLM puts aside such criticism. "There's a tendency for folks to equate an effort to speed up time frames with less public involvement and less environmental protection. But that's not necessarily the case," says Pete Culp, the BLM's assistant secretary for minerals and resource protection. "We're trying to show that it isn't really a matter of streamlining, it's about cooperation and communication."

But if the Dome Plateau project is any indication, it remains to be seen whether the BLM has the legal room to maneuver between executive direction and environmental law. And the test for whether cooperation and communication will apply in this case is coming soon. The Interior Department has directed the IBLA to fast-track its review of SUWA's Dome Plateau appeal. A decision is expected by August.

May 13, 2002

BUSH'S ENERGY PUSH MEETS UNINTENDED CONSEQUENCES

by Jon Margolis

⁊ℓℓ

AS SUBSTANCES GO, natural gas doesn't have much substance. Oh, it's real enough. Mishandled, it can explode. Properly handled, it can heat homes, power vehicles, and generate electricity. But being a gas, it lacks solidity. Unless it is liquefied, you cannot see it, much less grasp it.

Natural gas, then, is sort of like money, which these days can be seen and touched only in its "liquid" form of currency. Or like politics, which is also difficult to grasp.

All of which fits the war now raging over drilling for natural gas in the public domain of the Rocky Mountain West. It is a war with substantive consequences—whether the country will have enough affordable energy; how much protection will be granted to the land, water, and wildlife. But it is also a war launched by people who stand to make a great deal of money. And so far, it has been dominated by politics.

To appreciate the substance-politics nexus here, it is only necessary to consider the difference between what President George W. Bush said from one May to the next. Bush effectively declared this war on May 18, 2001, with an Executive Order

(Number 13212) proclaiming that "increased production of energy...is essential to the well-being of the American people," and that it was therefore "the policy of this administration that executive departments and agencies—shall take appropriate action—to expedite (energy production) projects."

Translated from the bureaucratese, Bush was saying that more coal, oil, and natural gas ought to be produced almost everywhere on the public domain.

One year and 11 days later, standing next to his brother, Gov. Jeb Bush of Florida, the president proposed spending $235 million to buy back oil and natural gas rights on some 765,000 acres of federal land in that state.

Officially, Bush did not rewrite his executive order to say "increased production of energy is essential to the well-being of the American people except in states where environmental views prevail, my brother is running for re-election, and I'm going to need all the help I can get in 2004." But, translated from the bureaucratese, that's the gist of it.

Meet the "Energy Impact Statement"

The debate over energy development in the Rockies contains obvious echoes of the one over drilling for oil in Alaska's Arctic

National Wildlife Refuge. One side says the energy is needed immediately. The other says, no, it isn't, because there isn't all that much of it, because ample reserves exist elsewhere, and besides, that's a very special place.

Echoes, but also differences. Governmentally, the Bush administration needs no congressional approval to allow the drill rigs to roll in the Rockies. Politically, the Arctic Refuge was famous, while few Americans have heard of the Rocky Mountain Front or the Red Desert in Wyoming, rendering it harder to mobilize opposition.

And developers and the administration have left little doubt that they want to drill in Wyoming's Jack Morrow Hills, Montana's Rocky Mountain Front, Utah's Dome Plateau just outside of Arches National Park, and other places of "ecological, geological, and wildlife wonder" in the words of Stephen C. Torbit, the senior scientist at the Rocky Mountain Natural Resource Center of the National Wildlife Federation.

To the extent that the Bush executive order did not convey that message, the first official act pursuant to it did. Seven months after the president issued the order—in Washington, that's quick—the acting director of the Bureau of Land Management issued an "Instruction Memorandum" (Number 2002-053, if you're keeping track) instructing her underlings to prepare a "Statement of Adverse Energy Impact" every time "your decisions or actions will have a direct or indirect adverse impact on energy development, production, supply and/or distribution."

In effect, the administration had created an "energy impact statement," comparable to the environmental impact statements (EIS) required (but by law, not administrative order) for most development projects on federal land.

Applications to drill, pump, and pipe may be denied. But to anyone who understands how bureaucracies work, the message of the executive order and the instruction memorandum is clear: The burden of argument is on the denier, and the BLMer who wants commendations on his/her personnel file will deny very carefully and quite rarely.

THE BLMER WHO WANTS COMMENDATIONS ON HIS/HER PERSONNEL FILE WILL DENY [ENERGY APPLICATIONS] VERY CAREFULLY AND QUITE RARELY.

This pro-producer mindset has been ordained despite evidence from the pro-producer National Petroleum Council that the country has more than enough natural gas to last for decades, even without drilling in those sensitive areas.

POLITICS IS FULL OF SURPRISES

As usual, policy changes have consequences. The BLM is fast-tracking lease applications, drilling permits, and seismic studies. And when the White House Task Force on Energy Product Streamlining completes its work in November, the tracking is likely to get faster yet.

For example, there are now roughly 60,000 wells producing natural gas onshore in the continental United States. The industry has proposed drilling more than 60,000 new ones in Montana and Wyoming over the next ten years. What is on the drawing board, obviously, is a quantum leap in the number of natural gas wells.

Most of these are coalbed methane wells. The good news

about coalbed methane is that most of it is shallower—hence easier to get at—than most natural gas. The bad news is that the process for getting it out of ground requires pumping dirty water out of the coal seams to release the methane. "Pump and dump," is what some call it, and it isn't just the usual environmentalist suspects who are upset about it. The Izaak Walton League of America, a most establishment fraternity of fly-fishers, complained last October that this runoff could contaminate wetlands, poisoning waterfowl and wildlife.

"We want to make sure we come out of this process with fish and wildlife resources intact," said Jeff Fleming, the league's conservation director. In that effort, the league has joined forces with Trout Unlimited, and with the big game hunters of the North American Grouse Partnership and the Wildlife Management Institute. Members of these organizations tend to be upper-income Republicans, the kind who can get their senators on the phone.

This is only one of the political complexities facing the administration. Its own Environmental Protection Agency ruled that the Environmental Impact Statement for some of the proposed development in Wyoming's Powder River Basin was inadequate. Though the federal government holds rights to the gas, most of the surface there is privately owned, and while some of the ranchers don't mind coal-water solution dumped on their fields, some do.

Enough do, apparently, to make Rep. Barbara Cubin, Wyoming's very conservative, pro-development, Republican congresswoman, consider the wisdom of laws giving surface owners the right to limit, if not prohibit, drilling on their land.

"She doesn't have a position," for or against such proposals, said Cubin spokesman Bryan Jacobs. "She's trying to invoke a dialogue between people. Maybe there need to be laws to protect ranchers."

But so far, the Bush administration seems more concerned with protecting natural gas companies than protecting ranchers. And natural gas companies are doing what any other business would do while its friends hold power. They are seeking maximum opportunity with minimum restraint, because the restraints cost money, and are a pain in the neck.

The industry is already getting some of what it wants. Whether it will get it all will not be determined at least until November, when the White House Task Force on Energy Product Streamlining completes its work, no doubt not before November 5. That's Election Day.

September 2, 2002

CLINTON-ERA MONUMENTS WEATHER COURT CHALLENGE

by Joshua Zaffos

A FEDERAL COURT HAS RULED that former President Clinton did, in fact, have the authority to create national monuments in four Western states.

The Blue Ribbon Coalition, an off-road vehicle users group, and the Mountain States Legal Foundation had opposed the designation of six monuments in Arizona, Colorado, Oregon, and Washington. National monument designation limits motorized use as well as logging, mining, and energy development. In a lawsuit, the groups claimed Clinton exceeded his authority under the Antiquities Act of 1906, and that the law could only be used to protect cultural artifacts, not the lands themselves.

Interior Secretary Gale Norton is former lead attorney at Mountain States Legal Foundation, and the Bush administration has threatened to dismantle and weaken monuments. Concerned that the government would not defend the designations, environmental groups intervened in the suit.

Environmentalists' fears were confirmed when, in its defense of the case, the Bush administration argued that the courts have no power to review national monument designations—a claim that would have allowed the president to shrink or do away with the national monuments without any judicial review.

"(The government) was trying to hit a home run against the Antiquities Act," says Jim Angell, an Earthjustice attorney.

On October 18, the U.S. Court of Appeals in Washington, D.C., dismissed the challenge, declaring, "At no point has Mountain States presented factual allegations that would occasion further review of the president's actions."

November 25, 2002

BUSH TURNS BLM INTO ENERGY MACHINE

by Charles Levendosky

IN NOVEMBER, QUIETLY and without fanfare, Acting Director of the Bureau of Land Management Nina Rose Hatfield created a National Energy Office to implement President Bush's energy policy.

Its sole purpose, according to BLM documents, is to expedite drilling and mining on public lands.

Last May, Bush issued Executive Order 13212, which stresses that it will be his administration's policy to increase production and transmission of energy. And all public-lands agencies are ordered to expedite their review of permits for energy-related projects.

By creating the new office, a stark message has been sent to state BLM directors: Exploration of energy resources is now the primary goal of the agency. To reinforce the primacy of energy-related activities, the national BLM office sent state BLM directors a set of rules regarding decisions or actions that would adversely impact energy development.

According to a December 12 memorandum from Acting Director Hatfield, state BLM offices must justify in writing any decision that denies an oil or gas or coal permit. They must explain why the "energy-related use cannot co-exist with other multiple uses of the land."

The offices must also make a judgment concerning the impact of any adverse energy decision "in regards to production lost, missed exploration opportunities, etc., as well as steps taken to offset the losses." With a heavy hand, the memorandum tilts the balance of competing uses of the land and protection of wildlife habitat toward energy production.

The BLM's National Energy Office has set 43 tasks for itself, according to Director Erick Kaarlela. Tasks in Category 1 do not require regulations or legislation and should be completed within three to six months, according to BLM documents. Within that period, the agency intends to shorten the time frame for approving applications for permits to drill, to streamline procedures for obtaining coal leases and processing pending geothermal leases, and to remove obstacles to applications for energy-related rights-of-way.

Tasks that fall into Category 2 require action by the administration. One of the tasks outlined in this category states that the "BLM will look for opportunities to improve and streamline the management of the NEPA (National Environmental Policy Act) process for all energy resource proposals." The BLM targets the NEPA process for energy proposals only. Yet federal mandate requires the BLM to manage the public lands for multiple use while protecting the environmental integrity of those lands. No single use is supposed to be top dog—not energy production, not bird-watching, not cross-country skiing.

Category 3 tasks require regulatory action. Tasks outlined in this category include evaluating royalty rate reductions and other incentives for enhanced recovery of oil, policy changes relative to liability and reclamation, adopting a uniform policy to solve coal and coalbed methane conflicts and lowering royalty payments for the recovery of uneconomic or marginally economic coal resources.

Category 4 tasks require legislative action: reducing royalty rates for enhanced recovery of oil to extend the life of an oil field; determining the necessary steps for an environmentally sound development of oil in the Arctic National Wildlife Refuge; and amending the Mineral Leasing Act to streamline coal-lease operations.

The BLM's National Energy Office was created to be an in-house agent of the energy industry. Kaarlela reinforced that concept in a Feb. 1 interview. He considers the main function of his office to be "coordinating the activity on federal land that the bureau has a responsibility for managing." According to Kaarlela, "That ranges from leasing the land for energy development, approval of permits for energy development, including such things as rights-of-ways for pipelines and transmission of energy across federal land. We're looking at those sorts of things; rights-of-way for wind power and solar power would be part of that, also."

Kaarlela says the memorandum sent to state BLM offices "isn't meant in any way as a requirement to prevent or preclude decisions that may be contrary to energy development." Then Kaarlela gives it away: "It's just to ensure that people are aware of the president's executive order and that we have a way of tracking the activity of the Bureau."

The BLM doesn't have an office of snowmobiles and off-road vehicles or an office for downhill and cross-country skiing. If it did, a public outcry would be justified. But now, the BLM does have a National Energy Office. And that office is clearly exerting enormous influence in favor of the energy industry.

ROAD WARRIORS BACK
ON THE OFFENSIVE

by Michelle Nijhuis

୧୧

THE PRESS RELEASE COULDN'T have been blander. The "Final Rule on Conveyances, Disclaimers, and Correction Documents," announced by the Bureau of Land Management on Christmas Eve, sounded like little more than regulatory housekeeping. The rule, said the agency, was simply designed to "remove clouds of title to the lands in which the BLM no longer holds interest."

So why had the proposed rule received more than 17,000 public comments, most of them negative? Why did press releases from environmental groups use the words "bulldozers" and "national parks" in such uncomfortably quick succession?

The newly minted rule continues an old, ugly argument over roads on public lands. The tussle has already spawned a string of lawsuits, at least one arrest, and countless hours of overblown rhetoric. These days, a lot rides on its resolution.

The state of Utah has claimed rights-of-way for about 10,000 routes across federal lands, some within Grand Staircase-Escalante National Monument. Southeastern California's San Bernardino County has claimed about 5,000 miles of desert trails and roads, about half of them in the Mojave National Preserve.

On January 10, just days after the administration's final rule was officially adopted, commissioners in northwestern Colorado's Moffat County also took action: They adopted a resolution that claims rights-of-way for hundreds of miles of routes on public lands, including Dinosaur National Monument and areas proposed for wilderness designation by environmental groups.

Former Moffat County Commissioner T. Wright Dickinson, who stepped down from his post in January, says his county's position is simple. "These are valid existing rights that were granted by Congress," he says. "They're based on the most common-sense law that Congress ever passed."

> THE NEWLY MINTED RULE CONTINUES AN OLD, UGLY ARGUMENT OVER ROADS ON PUBLIC LANDS. THE TUSSLE HAS ALREADY SPAWNED A STRING OF LAWSUITS, AT LEAST ONE ARREST, AND COUNTLESS HOURS OF OVERBLOWN RHETORIC.

NEW LIFE FOR AN OLD LAW

That "common-sense law" dates back to 1866, when Congress passed the Lode Mining Act. Buried in the act was a single sentence known as Revised Statute 2477, or "RS 2477" for short: "(T)he right of way for the construction of highways over public lands, not reserved for public uses, is hereby granted."

In those days, the acres "reserved for public uses," such as parks, were almost nonexistent, so local governments had more or less blanket permission to build and maintain roads on public land.

More than a century later, the 1976 Federal Land Policy and Management Act repealed RS 2477 and established more stringent restrictions. The new law contained a catch, however: If states, counties, or even individuals could prove that a road had been in continuous use since before 1976—or before the land was reserved for a park or other protected area—they could still claim it under RS 2477.

This caveat remained relatively obscure until 1988, when President Reagan's Interior Secretary, Donald Hodel, issued a new official policy on RS 2477. His loose interpretation of the statute said even the most primitive paths could be claimed as rights-of-way.

The Hodel policy was welcome news in southern Utah, where county governments were fighting their state's growing wilderness movement. Since wilderness areas must be roadless, county commissioners began using RS 2477 claims to literally tear holes in proposed wilderness areas, as well as existing wilderness areas and parks.

The tactic proved popular throughout the West. Some counties even sent bulldozers and road crews to widen and pave routes on public land.

In the mid-1990s, Interior Secretary Bruce Babbitt attempted to tighten the federal road policy, but the Utah congressional delegation successfully pushed for a moratorium on all RS 2477 policy changes. Babbitt responded with a moratorium of his own, blocking his department from processing nearly all RS 2477 claims.

'A ONE-TWO PUNCH'

That's how things stood on Christmas Eve, when the bland BLM press release appeared on the Internet. Under the new final rule, counties and other "entities" are eligible to apply to the agency for a "disclaimer of interest" on a piece of disputed property, such as a road. The BLM will then decide if the federal government is willing to give up its claim to the property.

Environmentalists fear the rule will make it quicker and easier for counties to get federal support for their RS 2477 road claims—and make it tougher to fight the claims in court.

BLM spokesman Jeff Holdren says the rule does provide "another option" for these RS 2477 claimants. But is it a way around the existing Babbitt moratorium? "I just don't know that yet."

It may be a moot point, as the moratorium's days are likely numbered. In a speech to the Alaska Resources Development Council in late November, Deputy Secretary of the Interior J. Steven Griles promised that his department would issue a new policy on RS 2477. Though Interior Secretary Gale Norton isn't likely to return to the Hodel era, her policy will surely be more relaxed than the thwarted Babbitt proposal.

"We're going to see a one-two punch here," says Ted Zukoski, an attorney for Earthjustice in Denver. The combined effect of the final rule and the new policy, he says, could be enormous. "We're going to see thousands of proposals, and we're going to have to fight them route by route."

February 3, 2003

MONUMENT PRESENTS
A MANAGEMENT MORASS

by Mitch Tobin

⁓

WHEN PRESIDENT BILL CLINTON'S pen stroke created the Ironwood Forest National Monument on the edge of Tucson, Arizona, it received a relatively warm welcome from many residents here. But if Ironwood has offered one lesson since then, it's that with the West's population on the rise, even a monument with public support can turn into a hornet's nest.

Clinton's proclamation, delivered on June 9, 2000, gave new protection to one of the most biologically diverse sections of the Sonoran Desert—a vulnerable ecosystem that has been steadily encroached on by suburbia. But it's also made the monument's craggy mountains and ancient trees more popular with both locals and out-of-state tourists, raising fears that the new monument will be "loved to death."

Some visitors come to Ironwood to ride 4x4s, off-road vehicles, and dirt bikes. Others come for target practice with handguns and high-powered rifles. These activities don't mix well, and even relatively low-impact activities, such as hiking, may soon be restricted to protect the monument's rare wildlife species.

As Ironwood approaches its third birthday, the Bureau of

Land Management is just now preparing to draft its management plan for the 129,000-acre monument. The agency says it will stick to its multiple-use tradition, attempting to balance environmental protection with the increasing demand for public access. But that may be easier said than done.

"There are no cookbook solutions or quick fixes to these things," says monument manager Tony Herrell.

COMPETING USES

As with the Grand Staircase-Escalante National Monument in Utah, Ironwood will continue to host some livestock grazing; Clinton's declaration preserved current grazing leases and continues to regulate them by existing laws. But with more visitors, ranchers may have a more difficult time.

One immediate threat to ranchers is local residents and their guns. Stray bullets have defoliated hillsides, whizzed by ranchers, and prompted calls for a total ban on shooting at Ironwood. Rancher Jesus Arvizu, whose family settled in the area in 1847, has put up "No Shooting" signs only to see them shot down. He says 24 of his cattle have been shot in recent months.

"I'm not against hunting or anything," says Arvizu, who ranches about 40,000 acres within Ironwood, "but when you're just out here drinking beers and shooting up signs, you call that safe?" Another unresolved issue is how much grazing to allow on monument land designated as critical habitat for the endangered pygmy owl, a species that has stalled development in parts of urban Tucson.

Hikers, too, may have to make concessions for imperiled wildlife, such as the desert bighorn sheep. Many environmental activists support closing popular hiking trails that go through areas where the sheep breed and lamb, pointing out that sheep herds in nearby mountains have suffered after hikers and their dogs moved in.

Regulations on recreation might help the bighorn sheep, but other management restrictions in high-profile areas like the monument can sometimes hurt the species, says Brian Dolan of the Arizona Desert Bighorn Sheep Society. In Tucson's signature mountain range, the Santa Catalinas, opposition to prescribed burning allowed brush to grow thicker, creating hiding places for predators and contributing to the local bighorn herd's demise, he says.

"I can just see the uproar if we want to do prescribed burns of ironwood trees in Ironwood National Monument," Dolan says. "We're going to get into the mindset that we need overly restrictive preservation measures, and end up doing more harm than good."

ANOTHER KIND OF ROAD WAR

So far, local BLM officials have earned praise from environmentalists for taking conservation seriously. The BLM is forcing the Phoenix-based Asarco's Silver Bell mine, which is nearly surrounded by Ironwood, to remove an illegal road, pipeline, and power line from the monument and revegetate the area. Asarco had asked for a land swap that would have given it 400 acres of monument land.

But activists are getting mixed messages from Washington. Clinton's Ironwood proclamation limited off-road vehicles and other motorized uses to existing roads. Interior Secretary Gale

Norton has since given individual monument managers more discretion over road closures, making it possible for the BLM to keep user-created roads and trails open to the public.

That may be a significant change at Ironwood. The monument already has more than 600 miles of roads that fragment wildlife habitat, says Julie Sherman of the Sierra Club. "Our argument is that nothing that was created since the proclamation should be there," she says. Parties involved in the road issue say some routes will inevitably be closed in the management plan, especially redundant roads and those crossing sensitive habitat. But the BLM is unlikely to close all user-created routes, as some environmentalists would like.

Many of the newest roads have been created by one of Ironwood's biggest, but illegal, user groups: people coming north from Mexico. Although Ironwood is nearly 60 miles from the border, it lies at the north end of a popular route through the Tohono O'odham reservation. Much of the illegal human traffic shifted to routes such as this after enforcement was stepped up in border cities in the mid-1990s.

Immigrants and drug smugglers are increasingly using the monument as a transfer point, blazing new roads that are later used by legal visitors. "It's very innocent for anyone to come out there later and travel on one of those road established by smugglers," says Ironwood manager Herrell.

Ironwood has just two law enforcement officers to patrol its 295 square miles. They've been shot at and had their vehicles rammed by smugglers, Herrell says. Additional officers have sometimes been brought in, but monument officials want more help on a permanent basis.

But some local environmentalists are dubious about how much support monument managers will receive from Washington. "There hasn't been a follow-up by the Bush administration to support management of these monuments," says Daniel Patterson, desert ecologist for the Tucson-based Center for Biological Diversity. "Their vision would be for the monuments to exist on paper only."

April 14, 2003

WHY I FIGHT: THE COMING
GAS EXPLOSION IN THE WEST

by Tweeti Blancett

✿

HERE'S WHAT I ONCE BELIEVED: that if the president knew about the damage done to our land by the energy industry, the damage would cease.

I once believed that if you could show that industry can extract gas without damaging land right near us—as it does on the Southern Ute Indian Reservation, and on Ted Turner's Vermijo Ranch—that those examples would be followed by every company.

Believing that, I went to Washington, D.C., in August 2002, and met with Kathleen Clarke, who runs the Bureau of Land Management; I met with Rebecca Watson, a Montanan high in the Department of Interior; I met with V.A. Stephens, who is with the Council on Environmental Quality; and I met with the New Mexico congressional staffs. I told them all that gas drilling could be done right, but that it was being done wrong. I begged them to enforce existing regulations.

I came home to the small town of Aztec, N.M., and waited for change. I'm still waiting. I suppose not everyone can waltz into Washington and get that kind of entree. But I ran George

Bush's 2000 campaign in my part of New Mexico. I ran Sen. Pete Domenici's campaign in my county in 1996. Our family has been on the land here for six generations and going on three centuries. We graze cattle on 17 square miles of Bureau of Land Management, state, and our private land.

We once ran 600 cows on those 35,000 acres. Today, we can barely keep 100 cows. Grass and shrubs are now roads, drill pads, or scars left by pipeline paths. We have trouble keeping our few cows alive because they are run over by trucks servicing wells each day, or they are poisoned when they lap up the sweet antifreeze leaking out of unfenced compressor engines.

> OUR FAMILY HAS BEEN ON THE LAND HERE FOR SIX GENERATIONS AND GOING ON THREE CENTURIES.

I have not taken this quietly. I have been on a mission for 16 years. In the beginning, I wanted to save the 400-acre farm and the adjacent piece of wild land in northwest New Mexico that I care most about. That's not much out of 35,000 acres. My family thought I was nuts. My son was a senior in high school, and resisted my attempts to enlist him. My husband said I was wasting my time.

They knew I was going against an industry that sharpened its teeth chewing on little people. They thought industry had the upper hand, legally speaking. But I believed industry had the upper hand because it threatened and intimidated. I once met Rosa Parks. I thought: If that little lady could sit, alone, in the front of a bus filled with hostile passengers, then I could act to protect where I live.

Gradually, I came to see why everyone else thought I was nuts. All of San Juan County in northern New Mexico has been leased for 50 years to gas companies. Our fathers and grandfathers signed these "perpetual" leases long ago, when the gas companies were owned and run by neighbors. The rest of the land is federally managed.

I ONCE MET ROSA PARKS. I THOUGHT: IF THAT LITTLE LADY COULD SIT, ALONE, IN THE FRONT OF A BUS FILLED WITH HOSTILE PASSENGERS, THEN I COULD ACT TO PROTECT WHERE I LIVE.

The industry claims its right to underground minerals trumps our rights to the surface. We don't deny their rights. We just say that we also have rights. Unfortunately for us and our cows and the wildlife, we are on top of unimaginable wealth, in the form of coalbed methane. Each year, our small, rural, and fairly poor county produces $2.4 billion, and most of that money flows right out of here.

My 400 acres sit at the heart of this wealth. Nevertheless, several of us last fall locked the gates to our private land. We have not denied access to those who have leases. But we now control the access. We were tired of being told by the companies that "someone else" had killed the cow, or the deer, or drove across freshly reseeded land. Now we know who is on our land, and when.

It's perfectly logical and legal to control access to private land, except in gas country. So the companies pulled us into court. This, it turned out, was not a bad thing. We found out that industry doesn't have the rights it says it has. And when we go to court, we don't go alone. We bring our rancher friends. We bring our environmental friends—friends we never dreamed of having. We bring pictures of the surface damage—pictures that are so bad other states use them to show what happens when you trust industry and the BLM to "do the right thing."

We've been in more newspapers than I can count. We've been in *People* magazine. We've been on Tom Brokaw's TV news program. This natural gas boom has become a Western plague. In conservative Wyoming, home to Vice President Dick Cheney, the reaction against coalbed methane helped elect a Democratic governor.

But this isn't a partisan issue. We had as much trouble under Clinton as we do under Bush. This is a campaign-contribution problem. They give more than we can.

At times, it seems hopeless. Then I hear from people facing similar situations in Colorado, in Montana, in Wyoming, in Utah. Many are like us—conservative, Republican, pro-free enterprise people. Others are environmentalists, or just care about land and animals.

Shortly, there will be a huge natural gas explosion, but it won't be pipelines or gas wells that blow. The explosion will come from the average Westerner, who is tired of being used by the oil and gas industry, with the help of state and federal officials.

June 9, 2003

ACT V

A Final Act Yet
to be Written

Un-named slot canyon, north side of
Escalante River drainage

INTERIOR VIEW V

by Ed Marston

🖋

MARSTON: The 20 United States senators from the West have always seemed incredibly powerful, and yet over the past few years, they seem to be unable to block initiatives like the monuments, like the roadless moratorium. Have they lost power?

BABBITT: Well, they haven't lost power. It's a question of how they exercise it. I think the monuments are one example. These actions have enormous public support. (Take, for example) the Grand Canyon expansion—the Parashant National Monument, down in Arizona. The statewide polls in Arizona came back with 75 percent support. Now, at that point, I think, a goodly number of Westerners said, "We're opposed," but they weren't about to waste a lot of chips in a knock-down, drag-out battle, representing the commodity folks, in the face of 75 percent public approval. They also know that if they want to overturn these things, they must deal, as is entirely proper, with the congressional delegations from California and the rest of the country, where people feel somewhat differently.

MARSTON: What was your relationship with the environmentalists?

BABBITT: I would say it was a love-hate relationship. The environmentalists' job is to move the goalpost. Whenever you get near them (the goal posts), they celebrate briefly, and then they say you haven't done enough. It's part of the job. I must say, the one big transformation coming on is (that) the environmental movement is going regional and going local and our great successes have been to get out on the landscape and get working on a particular problem. You don't look to Washington for an environmental group. You look for the environmental groups that are out on the land. And I think that part of the relationship has been especially productive and made a huge difference.

MARSTON: You often describe the West as a Kabuki drama. What does that mean?

BABBITT: What it means is that we tend to argue the future by simply adopting the costumes, the masks, and the rhetoric of the past, notwithstanding the fact that the West is a very different place, and each decade sort of reinvents itself and heads in new directions.

MARSTON: And do you think we are caught up in an endless cycle?

BABBITT: Well, it might be a longer cycle than I would have thought when I first went into public life 25 years ago. Basically the Western debate is between the commodity producers, who think of themselves as on a 19th century commons, that inexhaustible supply of forage, timber and minerals. And (then) there are a lot of new voices in the West: the environmental movement, the recreationists, urban areas looking for clean water supplies. And so it will continue.

But public lands really are a unique phenomenon. It is kind

of ironic that the United States of America, with our market-based economics, has seen fit to protect this large public-land base, and so it does set up some ideological conflict. You see it all the time from the Cato Institute and all these groups that say "it's an insult" to the Number One capitalist economy in the world that we have a public domain.

MARSTON: Twenty-nine percent of the country.

BABBITT: Yeah, we have lands held in common. The right-wingers are offended by the concept. But the fact is, Americans are pragmatic people, and they know from history that this public-land base is an extraordinary part of our heritage. If you go to Europe—if you want to go hunting, well, you'd better have a duke or an earl who is a friend, or be very rich, because there's nowhere else for a person to go; the land is all owned, fenced, and locked up. Americans have rejected that model, and I think they always will.

February 12, 2001

REOPENING THE WOUNDS
IN SOUTHERN UTAH

by Paul Larmer

I VISITED THE SPECTACULAR Grand Staircase-Escalante National Monument in 1996, when it was still a raw wound in the body politic of southern Utah. As I talked to people in the scattered, dusty towns around the almost 1.9 million-acre-monument, I found deep-seated anger. There was the rancher who predicted he would never again be allowed to graze cattle on the monument, and the local county commissioner, who condemned Bill Clinton for using the monument as a political chip to win green votes in the 1996 presidential election. There was plenty of talk of getting rid of the monument, through lawsuits or legislation.

But not everyone was so confrontational. In fact, after venting about "Bill Clinton's goddamn monument," some quietly told me that they felt the designation would bring new attention—and a badly needed economic shot in the arm—to their communities. They recognized something that the most entrenched opponents would not: The West had changed. Ranching, logging, and mining, the perceived mainstays of the southern Utah economy, were already shadows of their former selves. Tourism was on the rise, and a new monument would make it rise even faster.

Over time, this reality has become more accepted by people in southern Utah. More people are coming to the area, and new businesses have sprung up to accommodate them. The federal agency overseeing the monument, the Bureau of Land Management, has bolstered the local economy by increasing its staff and building new visitor facilities.

The monument has also bolstered the agency's legal obligation to protect the environment, which, in turn, has provided an opportunity for one fading industry of the traditional West to ride gracefully off into the sunset. Over the past several years, a number of ranchers have agreed to stop grazing sensitive lands within the monument in exchange for money or grazing rights on less-sensitive lands elsewhere. These buyouts and trades, brokered by Bill Hedden of the Grand Canyon Trust, have been good for the land and the people.

OLD WEST RESENTMENTS DIE HARDER THAN THE OLD WEST ITSELF.

Yet, Old West resentments die harder than the Old West itself. The election of George W. Bush and the swing back to Republican power have encouraged a few opportunists to reopen old wounds. In 2001, Canyon Country Rural Alliance, a group headed by former BLM staffer and state legislator Mike Noel, convinced administration officials to remove Kate Cannon, the very capable manager of the monument; her sin was that she had asked ranchers to remove their cattle from the monument a few weeks earlier than scheduled because of a severe drought. And now, the alliance has set in on the grazing retirement program in the name of defending the "custom and culture" of Escalante country—even verbally attacking the ranchers who have participated.

This swing back and forth from the New West to the Old reads like an eye-for-an-eye story from the Old Testament: Clinton used the monument designation as a blunt political tool to bolster his chances in the 1996 election, so it's only fair that the angry locals use an all-too-willing Bush administration to strike back. Right?

Wrong. Stories like this make for good headlines in the newspapers, but they represent a step backward for the West. The truth is that, as opportunistic as Clinton's late-inning designation might have been, it was a step forward for the economy and environment of southern Utah. The monument is here to stay, and no amount of harassment from the perpetually disgruntled will change that. Many locals are fed up with the acrimony

The West has changed, and it's time for southern Utahns to stand up to the bullies still railing against the monument and its staff. If they don't, the wounds will never heal, and everyone will lose out.

April 14, 2003

CHANGE COMES SLOWLY TO ESCALANTE COUNTRY

by Michelle Nijhuis

✿

KATE CANNON LOOKS LIKE SHE was born to work here. The spacious deputy superintendent's office, the trim Park Service uniform, the low-watt glow of self-assurance; she's got all the trappings of an accomplished bureaucrat. She's got the experience, too. She speaks nostalgically of long-ago summers spent at Isle Royale and Canyonlands, and of the fistful of parks she left behind during her climb up the agency ladder. This post at the Grand Canyon could easily be the high point of a successful career.

Cannon, though, has already had her dream job, and it wasn't with the National Park Service. Little more than a year ago, she was the proud manager of the Grand Staircase-Escalante National Monument in southern Utah—the first national monument overseen by the Bureau of Land Management.

The job demanded much more than a change of uniform. The almost 1.9 million-acre monument was intended not only for sightseeing and backpacking and scientific research, but also for limited grazing and oil and gas development. The monument aimed to manage all these uses carefully, for the long-term health of the land. Grand Staircase-Escalante also had a larger mission:

Its staff was to lead the way for 14 other, smaller BLM national monuments established during the Clinton administration. Together, the new monuments cover nearly 5 million acres, a small but significant share of the more than 260 million acres managed by the BLM.

It was a huge, high-stakes experiment for the BLM, and success required changing the very culture of the agency. For Cannon, it was a plum of a job. The redrock canyons were staggeringly beautiful, the research possibilities were endless, and the potential for a new, more conservation-oriented sort of multiple-use management was real and immediate. It was, she says, the most complex challenge of her career. The challenge was short-lived. In late 2001, after about three years in the manager's office, Cannon was offered a choice by her superiors: Take a post with the Park Service at the Grand Canyon, or move to Washington, D.C., and oversee an environmental impact statement for energy development on BLM lands.

IT WAS A HUGE, HIGH-STAKES EXPERIMENT FOR THE BLM, AND SUCCESS REQUIRED CHANGING THE VERY CULTURE OF THE AGENCY.

The decision wasn't difficult. By the end of the year, Cannon had packed up and moved south.

Cannon's abrupt departure, many say, has been chilling for the colleagues she left behind, and that fear has slowed the agency's massive effort to transform itself. How the Bureau of Land Management lost this highly qualified staffer, and also the momentum she and others brought with them, is a peculiar story of local grudges, presidential politics, and the nasty collision between them.

THOSE WHO LIVE NEAR the Escalante canyons call their home "the country," as if the canyon rims on the eastern horizon are the shores of an independent republic. "My family has always ranched in this country, and that's all I've ever wanted to do," some say. Or, "Before I got to the country, I was just a climbing bum." Or, "Him? He just hasn't been in this country long enough to understand it."

The most common expression, though, goes something like this: "I came to the country, and I fell in love at first sight."

No wonder. The canyons' smooth red rocks and green cottonwood oases and crooked slices of blue sky have an overpowering, almost narcotic beauty. Sometimes, in some places, this land doesn't just look like another country. It looks like another galaxy.

So it's hard to find a neutral person around here. Loyalties are cherished for generations, and memories are as long and deep as nearby Glen Canyon. Nearly everyone loves the land, knows it well, and is dead sure what should and shouldn't be done with it.

Maybe that's why the Southern Utah Wilderness Alliance, the state's most aggressive and influential environmental group, got its start here a couple of decades ago, and why these small towns have also produced some of the region's most reactionary county commissioners. The generation-long struggle between environmentalists and their foes in Escalante country has been nothing less than a holy war. Though it's been mostly a battle of words, casualties have included cows (shot), cabins (burned), bulldozers (sabotaged), and the Burr Trail, known as one of the most spectacular backcountry drives in the world (paved).

On September 18, 1996, then-President Clinton forced this complicated, contentious little nation to face the rest of the world. By establishing the Grand Staircase-Escalante National Monument, Clinton opened the debate over the Escalante country's future to a national audience.

The surprise proclamation was a gigantic victory for environmentalists, who had been trying for years to block a proposed coal mine on the Kaiparowits Plateau. The monument, which prevented new mineral leases on its lands, effectively squelched the project.

Others in Escalante country were less than pleased. Remember the high school students who released dozens of black balloons, the residents who grimly set fire to an effigy of Clinton? These were the folks who'd grown up angry at the government, infuriated by the gradual tightening of grazing and logging restrictions on the surrounding public land. To them, the monument was just another example of federal meddling.

"The land wasn't ours, but we felt like it was," says former Kanab Mayor Karen Alvey. "It was as if we'd adopted a child, then been told we were no longer needed."

Frustration about the monument has flared up regularly in recent years, and its expression has often been personal and threatening. In the town of Escalante, some tied effigies of backpackers to the hoods of their pickup trucks, then lined up their vehicles on the town's main drag. When a couple of outspoken environmental activists from Berkeley, California, moved to town, their support of wilderness and opposition to a local reservoir project earned them repeated visits from vandals.

IN THE MIDDLE OF THIS boiling stew of resentments sat the Bureau of Land Management, freshly anointed by Clinton as a manager of national monuments. The agency, and the monument staff in particular, faced massive pressures from above and below, inside and out. Opponents in the local communities were mired in their own fury.

Environmentalists, though pleased about the president's proclamation, were wary of the BLM's livestock-and-mining past. High-level Park Service staffers felt they should have been the ones to manage this world-class piece of land. And though many within the BLM were flattered and excited by the new responsibility, some of its old guard resented the exhortation to change.

The Clinton administration did its best to shore up the monument and the near-friendless agency. Kate Cannon's predecessor, Jerry Meredith, got a $5 million budget in 1997 and a "dream team" of about 20 high-powered planners from the BLM and other state and federal agencies.

By the end of 1999, the team had come up with a management plan that emphasized scientific research and the primitive, "frontier" nature of the land. There would be no Park Service-style visitor center inside monument boundaries, no parking lots, no new paved roads.

Though grazing, recreation, and most other uses would be more closely watched than they had been, any additional restrictions would be based on existing law.

The management plan got mostly good reviews from environmentalists. "They did a very good job of developing a management plan that was true to the (presidential) proclamation," says Pam Eaton of The Wilderness Society's Four Corners office.

Even local critics started to unbend a little. The monument had begun hiring a steady stream of local high-school interns, and town and county politicians started to talk about making lemonade out of lemons. Kane County Commissioner Joe Judd, who had been outraged by the proclamation, realized the monument could and should benefit his county. He began traveling to Washington, D.C., to stump for federal funds, and he even became friendly with the likes of Clinton's Interior secretary, Bruce Babbitt.

Judd says he's done his best to forget his initial anger: "I tell people that if I try really hard, I can remember the monument (proclamation). But I don't choose to."

Dell LeFevre, one of the Garfield County commissioners who championed the paving of the Burr Trail, isn't quite so sanguine.

IT WAS A CHICKENSHIT TRICK, AS UNDERHANDED AS YOU CAN GET.

"It was a chicken-shit trick, as underhanded as you can get," he says without hesitation. But the monument has, at least indirectly, helped make his life a little bit easier.

Long before Clinton's proclamation, the BLM had been gradually restricting LeFevre's grazing allotment along the Escalante River. Fewer cattle on the riverbanks meant thicker willows, and the canyon was becoming tougher to navigate on horseback. One day, miles from home, LeFevre's horse punched through the roof of a beaver den, fell, and pinned him firmly to the ground. His horse was unable to right itself, so LeFevre lay there for four or five hours, staring up at the blue sky and racking his brain for an escape.

LeFevre had just resigned himself to shooting and butchering the horse when he remembered the long-ago advice of a mule-skinner acquaintance. He rummaged in his bag, pulled out a warm can of Pepsi, and carefully poured a few drops into the horse's ear. The horse started, shifting just enough for LeFevre to scramble out and start extricating his horse.

"After that," he says, "I thought, 'What am I doing in this river?'" LeFevre called Bill Hedden, the director of the Grand Canyon Trust's Moab, Utah, office. Since 1998, Hedden had been quietly negotiating with interested ranchers, offering to buy out and eventually retire their permits along the Escalante River. LeFevre traded his permit in the river for part of an allotment on the Kaiparowits Plateau, a decision he says was good for both his business and his disposition.

LeFevre is a larger-than-life figure: a veteran county commissioner, the father of 14 adopted kids, and one of only two or three people in the entire county to make a full-time living off his cattle. His unexpected decision helped dampen the community's wrath about the monument.

Just as things were looking—well, not peaceful, but more or less quietly resigned—a stack of butterfly ballots in Florida were counted and recounted, and national politics landed on the shores of Escalante country once again.

"I'LL BET THEY TOLD YOU they were making lemonade out of lemons," says Mike Noel sarcastically, speaking of LeFevre, Judd, and others. Noel is a recently elected Republican state legislator and a former BLM staffer; he spent 22 years working in the Kanab field office, the last of them as project director for the Kaiparowits coal mine proposal. He hates the monument, and he can't stand the locals who have started to come to terms with it. Of all the people in Escalante country, monument supporters and opponents alike, Noel is one of a handful who still thinks the monument can be overturned.

Noel is one of the leaders of the Canyon Country Rural Alliance, a group formed from a defunct chapter of People for the USA. Though few of the leaders of the group are full-time cattlemen, they're determined to keep the sinking industry afloat — even if it means bashing the ranchers who choose to deal with the Grand Canyon Trust.

"It doesn't matter if the ranchers want to do it," says Noel. "It just doesn't matter. They're selling their heritage for a mess of pottage."

LeFevre has heard such arguments more than a few times. "I've caught hell for this," he says of his decision to work with the Grand Canyon Trust. "Not from ranchers, but from those who are going to save the world." For once, he's not talking about environmentalists.

Many residents, like LeFevre, consider the Canyon Country Rural Alliance extremist. But just before the 2000 presidential election, alliance leaders got an unexpectedly dramatic boost from Mother Nature.

The summer of 2000 was the third summer of severe drought in Escalante country; in the monument, even the sagebrush was dying. Kate Cannon, who had stepped into the manager's job in

1998, took the advice of her range staff and warned all the ranchers on the monument that they might have to pull their cows off early. By mid-August, 80 to 90 percent of the forage was gone, and most ranchers had taken their cows off the land. Cannon ordered the remaining three ranchers to remove their cows by September 1.

Ranchers Gene Griffin, Quinn Griffin, and Mary Bulloch refused to budge. In October, Cannon sent agency wranglers and a helicopter to find and impound the mostly wild cattle, and the ranchers became immediate heroes of the wise-use movement. Followed by a crew of supporters, the trio traveled to Salina, Utah, where the BLM had taken the cattle for sale. It's not clear what happened next, but by the end of the day the local county sheriff had allowed the Griffins and Bulloch to open the sale-lot gate, load the animals into their trucks, and take off down the freeway for Arizona.

THERE'S NOTHING LIKE BEING A COWBOY IN THE MIDDLE OF SOCIETY, IS THERE?

Mary Bulloch, who lives in a cramped trailer just south of the Utah state line, remembers the showdown fondly. "It was real Western around here for a while," she says with a smile. "I got calls from all over the place, telling me congratulations, and I said, 'Yep, there's nothing like being a cowboy in the middle of society, is there?'"

The cattle dustup, combined with the results of the 2000 election, got Kane County feeling feisty all over again. "I saw that map with all the red squares," says Noel, referring to the

Republican sweep in the Rocky Mountains, "and I thought, 'Finally, rural America is going to have a voice.'"

In spite of the Canyon Country Rural Alliance's high hopes, and the swell of local encouragement they got after the presidential election, the Grand Staircase-Escalante National Monument didn't disappear along with President Clinton.

So Noel and his allies started in on Kate Cannon. Her enforcement of agency regulations—crystallized during the confrontation with the renegade ranchers—represented everything they disliked about the BLM's new attitude. They complained loudly to the Utah congressional delegation, and some even traveled to Washington, D.C., in the summer of 2001 to meet with then-Deputy Assistant Secretary of the Interior Tom Fulton.

"There was a drumbeat of criticism directed at her by Mike Noel and others," says David Alberswerth, a former Interior staffer who now directs The Wilderness Society's Bureau of Land Management program. "She was clearly singled out by disaffected local people, and they definitely had a great deal of influence."

By December 2001, the disaffected had gotten their way. Fulton says he doesn't recall a discussion of Cannon during the meeting in Washington, and says Cannon's transfer was "an internal BLM decision." Others inside and outside government offices, however, say the transfer order came from a high level in the Interior Department. The administration, some say privately, was eager to placate the monument opponents they'd wooed during the presidential campaign.

IN THE MONUMENT OFFICES, housed in an old middle school in Kanab, new monument manager Dave Hunsaker is good-naturedly doing his homework. For the past couple of weeks, he's been exchanging letters to the editor with Kane County commissioner Mark Habbeshaw—the latest skirmish in the continuing brouhaha over the Grand Canyon Trust grazing retirements. "We are tenacious, if nothing else," Hunsaker says wryly.

Kate Cannon's successor doesn't try to pretend that his job is an easy one. "Kate tried very hard to follow the (management) plan, and the counties had no one else to zero in on," he says. "I, too, am finding that I get zeroed in on."

Hunsaker hopes the arguments in Escalante country will someday target policies, not individuals. To that end, he's trying to smooth out relationships with the monument's most dogged critics. Hunsaker, a genial guy who jokes that he's been "married to the BLM for years," seems particularly well-qualified for the task.

Under Hunsaker's direction, much of the work in these offices—and on the land—has continued apace since Kate Cannon's departure. Sixty federal, state, and university scientists are conducting research in and around the monument, studying everything from fossil turtles to native seed banks to local oral history. The monument staff has organized several popular lecture series in the area, and two visitors' centers have opened in local communities.

HUNSAKER HOPES THE ARGUMENTS IN ESCALANTE COUNTRY WILL SOMEDAY TARGET POLICIES, NOT INDIVIDUALS.

Many in and out of the monument offices say the area's fossils, artifacts and natural resources are better protected under the monument designation, thanks to Grand Staircase-Escalante's substantial people power. Sage Sorensen, a longtime recreation planner for the agency, remembers when he was the only person keeping an eye on hikers, horses, and dirt bikes in the Escalante canyons. "It was way more than one person could handle," he remembers. He's now relieved to be part of a 20-member recreation staff.

But the effects of Cannon's sudden exit are still reverberating through these offices. Though new administrations routinely replace agency staff at the state and national levels, it's extremely unusual for someone on Cannon's rung to lose a job for political reasons. Her departure, along with the rapid-fire transfers of two other high-level BLM staffers—California BLM Desert District manager Tim Salt and Idaho state director Martha Hahn—was an unmistakable signal from the top. "Just seeing two or three moves like that was enough to scare people," says a former BLM official who asked not to be named. "Everyone is afraid they're going to get fired."

> EVERYONE IS AFRAID
> THEY'RE GOING
> TO GET FIRED.

So the monument staff is acting with a great deal more caution, especially when it comes to the more explosive local controversies. One of the most contentious—and hopelessly complicated—issues in Escalante country is the control of roads on public lands. The monument management plan cracked open that emotional debate, directing the agency to place "open" signs on the 908 miles of open monument roads and physically close the remaining routes. The monument transportation plan also requires that part of each year's budget be spent to block off and otherwise close old roads.

The agency has signed the open monument roads that lie within Kane County, but it hasn't placed signs on roads in neighboring Garfield County or closed any roads within the monument. Garfield County opposes the signing of roads on its side of the line, arguing that the county, not the federal government, controls the routes under Revised Statute 2477 of the Lode Mining Act of 1866. The Department of Interior halted processing of all RS 2477 road claims six years ago, and Hunsaker says the monument won't take action until Interior delivers new guidance on the issue. But many environmentalists say the BLM could start closing roads if it chose to.

"There's nothing—except fear of a lawsuit—that's keeping the BLM from enforcing its transportation plan," says Liz Thomas of the Southern Utah Wilderness Alliance.

The Grand Canyon Trust effort to retire four large grazing allotments along the Escalante River is also stuck in bureaucratic limbo. Though the group's trades and buyouts have already removed cattle from all or part of some 18 allotments in the watershed— deals that were reviewed and approved by the agency "without a peep" from the local communities, says Bill Hedden—the Canyon Country Rural Alliance is doing its best to block the most recent proposals.

The alliance's leaders have been encouraged by continuing local support; last year, several of them were elected to posts in town, county, and state government. They've also taken heart from public statements by top-drawer Bush administration officials. Interior Solicitor William Myers opined in late 2002 that the BLM could not completely exclude cattle from an allotment within a federal grazing district; BLM director Kathleen Clarke, a Utah native, recently told the Society for Range Management that "for too long, there's been an attitude that the only way to address range that is challenged is to remove the cattle."

In January 2003, the Utah state office of the BLM approved the environmental analyses of the four proposed grazing retirements, but said the long-term fate of all retirements would be decided in a monument-wide environmental impact statement on grazing. That document is behind schedule, and a final version is not expected until November 2004.

WHEN THE BUSH ADMINISTRATION GOT IN, IT WAS LIKE THROWING RED MEAT TO WOLVES.

Hedden, who has watched his once crowd-pleasing project devolve into a local bogeyman ("Don't Trust the Trust," says a common bumper sticker) says national politics and local resentment have been a deadly combination. "When the Bush administration got in, it was like throwing red meat to wolves," he says. "The attitude was, 'Now all we have to do is go for the throat, and make it so these new managers act like obedient sheep.'"

SO WHAT ABOUT THE NEW BLM? The national monuments, with Grand Staircase-Escalante as their flagship, were supposed to haul the agency into a brave new era. This administration is giving the BLM a not-so-gentle push in the opposite direction. What's a conservation-minded land manager to do?

She, or he, can take comfort in two words: national monument. No national monument has ever been overturned for purely political reasons (in fact, no one is quite sure how to do it) and, despite the best efforts of Mike Noel and his allies, the Grand Staircase-Escalante is unlikely to be an exception. Even the National Landscape Conservation System, the BLM's new office for national monuments and other special designations, has so far weathered the political storm.

Interior Secretary Gale Norton has been much less enthusiastic about the slew of new monuments than her predecessor, Bruce Babbitt, and she has announced some guidelines that could weaken protections at the more recent designations, but she has said that planning for all monuments will move ahead.

Grand Staircase-Escalante's budget has fluctuated slightly in recent years, but it was a substantial $6 million in fiscal year 2003. The other BLM monuments have much smaller budgets—ranging from less than half a million dollars for Kasha-Katuwe Tent Rocks National Monument in New Mexico to $2.4 million for the Upper Missouri River Breaks National Monument in eastern Montana—but they have still been able to hire some staff and start work on their management plans.

Some of these monuments also enjoy a lot more local support than Grand Staircase-Escalante, perhaps because of Babbitt's efforts to meet and negotiate with locals before Clinton continued his second-term monument tour. The popularity of some of these places has led to new problems, but a nearby fan base might help these monuments in unfriendly times.

So the lifespan of the BLM monuments is likely to be significantly longer than that of the Bush administration. The new, tougher BLM might not emerge as quickly as Clinton and Babbitt had hoped, but it could still be on its way.

Kate Cannon, for one, is hoping to be part of that agency. "If you're going to manage land, you need to go where the land is," she says. The hundreds of millions of acres managed by the BLM, she says, are becoming more and more important—not just for recreation, but also as open space.

> **THE NEW, TOUGHER BLM MIGHT NOT EMERGE AS QUICKLY AS CLINTON AND BABBITT HAD HOPED, BUT IT COULD STILL BE ON ITS WAY.**

Monument management shouldn't turn the BLM into a clone of the Park Service, she points out. "Even though I love parks, I don't want that model spread across the landscape," she says, gesturing out her office window toward the stuffed parking lots of Grand Canyon Village. Parks, she says, are an "easy introduction" to wild land. The BLM monuments can offer a vastly more varied experience.

Cannon and many other agency-watchers say the monuments demand something quite different of the BLM: stricter enforcement of the agency's own unique conservation regulations. The rules are based in long-standing law that declares multiple use, sustained yield, and environmental protection to be the agency's guiding principles. These values have often fallen prey to funding cuts and short staffing. The monuments, with their bulked-up budgets and specialized staff, have given the agency a chance to improve on history.

"We have a commitment to the public," says Cannon, "and I don't mean we the monument, I mean we the BLM. The monument is a small test of whether the BLM can meet its commitment to the public."

Just a short stroll from Cannon's office, on the southern lip of the Grand Canyon, President Clinton read the brief proclamation that established the Grand Staircase-Escalante National Monument. To some, that September afternoon felt like the victorious end of an exhausting battle. To others, it felt like the ultimate insult.

From nearly seven years out, that fateful afternoon looks a little bit different. It has turned out to be just the beginning of a difficult test for the BLM, and the beginning of a new and even more complicated debate over Escalante country. The outcome of that test, and the debate that accompanies it, depends on the people who love this extraordinary place: those who live here and those who visit from afar, those who work outside the agency and those who work within it. The true ending of this story, it seems, has yet to be written.

April 14, 2003

APPENDIX

NINETY YEARS OF THE ANTIQUITIES ACT

by Michelle Nijhuis

JUNE 1906—CONGRESS PASSES the Antiquities Act. It gives the president power to "declare by public proclamation…objects of historic and scientific interest that are situated upon the lands owned or controlled by the government of the United States to be national monuments, and may reserve as a part thereof parcels of land, the limits of which in all cases shall be confined to the smallest area compatible with proper care and management of the objects to be protected…"

SEPTEMBER 1906—President Theodore Roosevelt uses the new powers to designate Devils Tower National Monument in Wyoming. Later that year, he establishes the Petrified Forest and Montezuma Castle national monuments in Arizona, and the El Morro National Monument in New Mexico.

1908—Although the backers of the Antiquities Act had envisioned it as a way to protect relatively small archaeological sites, Roosevelt deep-sixes that assumption with the designation of 800,000 acres of the Grand Canyon as a national monument (it became a national park in 1919). An Arizona politician mounts a legal challenge to the monument, arguing that it's much larger than the "smallest area compatible with proper care and management," but the Supreme Court upholds the designation in 1920. Today, national monuments range in size from 10 acres to 12 million acres, and total about 70 million acres.

1909—With just hours left in his presidency, Roosevelt establishes Mount Olympus National Monument, now Olympic National Park. He begins a tradition of lame-duck monument proclamations.

1910-1928—Presidents Taft, Wilson, Harding and Coolidge establish monuments at a brisk pace, including Dinosaur, Zion and Bryce Canyon in Utah, Glacier Bay in Alaska, and the Statue of Liberty in upper New York Bay.

1933—Just before leaving office, Herbert Hoover establishes Saguaro, Black Canyon of the Gunnison, and Death Valley national monuments.

1943—Over the objections of Congress, Franklin Roosevelt designates Jackson Hole National Monument, setting off the first major controversy over the Antiquities Act. Wyoming Sen. Edward Robertson calls it a "foul, sneaking, Pearl Harbor blow," and Congress passes a series of bills abolishing the monument. None make it past Roosevelt's veto.

1950—Jackson Hole National Monument is incorporated into Grand Teton National Park. In exchange for congressional approval of the bill, Harry Truman signs a provision exempting Wyoming from the Antiquities Act.

1969—At the end of his term, Lyndon Johnson establishes Marble Canyon, now part of Grand Canyon National Park, and expands several other national monuments.

1978—In one day, Jimmy Carter creates 17 national monuments in Alaska—56 million acres' worth—after Congress fails to pass an Alaskan lands bill.

1996—From the rim of the Grand Canyon, Bill Clinton declares the Grand Staircase-Escalante in southern Utah a national monument. It's the largest national monument in the lower 48 states, and the 105th monument designated since the passage of the Antiquities Act. Although 29 of these monuments have since become national parks, the Escalante monument may not be on the same path. While almost all other monuments are overseen by the Park Service—with the exception of two Forest Service monuments—the Grand Staircase-Escalante is managed by the BLM.

2001—Just before leaving office, Bill Clinton establishes new national monuments including: The Sonoran Desert National Monument (AZ), the Upper Missouri River Breaks National Monument (MT), Carrizo Plain National Monument (CA), Kasha-Katuwe Tent Rocks National Monument (NM), Pompeys Pillar National Monument (MT), and the Minidoka Internment National Monument (ID).

CONTRIBUTOR PROFILES

JOAN BENNER, retired, was formerly wilderness and trails manager for the Sierra National Forest.

GAIL BINKLY is a contributor to Writers on the Range. She writes in Cortez, Colorado.

TWEETI BLANCETT is a rancher who has become an activist in Aztec, New Mexico.

KIRSTEN BOVEE was an intern at *High Country News*.

ADAM BURKE produced Radio High Country News from 1999 to 2003.

REBECCA CLARREN was associate editor of *High Country News*.

TONY DAVIS is a freelance writer out of New Mexico.

GREG HANSCOM is editor of *High Country News*.

BRENT ISRAELSEN writes for the *Salt Lake Tribune*.

MATT JENKINS is assistant editor of *High Country News*.

LISA JONES was an intern at *High Country News*.

CHARLES LEVENDOSKY is editorial page editor for Wyoming's *Casper Star-Tribune*.

JON MARGOLIS is a freelance writer who covers Washington, D.C. for *High Country News* from his home in Barton, Vermont.

ED MARSTON, formerly executive director of High Country Foundation and publisher of *High Country News*, is a Senior Journalist for *High Country News*.

EMILY MILLER was an intern at *High Country News*.

JAMIE MURRAY was an intern at *High Country News*.

MICHELLE NIJHUIS, formerly an editor of *High Country News*, is a freelance journalist residing in Paonia, Colorado.

ROCHELLE OXARANGO is sheep rancher who lives near the Craters of the Moon National Monument in Idaho

THOMAS MICHAEL POWER is a professor of economics and chairman of the Economics Department at the University of Montana.

RON SELDEN writes from Billings, Montana.

STEPHEN STUEBNER is a freelance writer from Boise, Idaho.

TIM SULLIVAN was an intern at *High Country News*.

DIANE SYLVAIN is a copyeditor and graphics designer for *High Country News*.

MITCH TOBIN is the environment writer at the *Arizona Daily Star* in Tucson, Arizona.

LARRY WARREN is a freelance writer from Park City, Utah.

TIM WESTBY was an intern at *High Country News*.

CHARLES F. WILKINSON is the Moses Lasky Professor of Law at the University of Colorado School of Law.

JOSHUA ZAFFOS, a former intern at *High Country News* who is a contributor to Writers on the Range, lives and writes in Paonia, Colorado.

INDEX

ABOUT THE EDITOR

Paul Larmer is executive director and publisher of *High Country News*. His first brush with *High Country News* came in the winter of 1984, when he became the paper's second intern since its arrival in Paonia, Colorado the year before. Prior to Paonia, *High Country News* had been headquartered in Lander, Wyoming since its inception in 1970. Back then, interns weren't paid, had to scrounge for their own housing, and used manual typewriters to bang out stories in an unheated hallway.

He rejoined the paper in 1992 after earning a Master's degree in Natural Resource Policy from the University of Michigan and serving as a media specialist for the national Sierra Club in San Francisco.

In 1997 he started Writers on the Range, *High Country News'* syndicated column service that is now carried by more than 80 newspapers in the West. In 2001 he became the editor of *High Country News*, and in November 2003 was appointed by the High Country Foundation Board as executive director and publisher.

Paul has a wife and two children, a dog, a horse, and has passion for bird watching, gardening, and basketball.

OUR COMMITMENT TO PRESERVING THE ENVIRONMENT

High Country News is committed to preserving ancient forests and natural resources. We have elected to print this title on Williamsburg Recycled Offset, which is 30% post-consumer recycled. As a result of our paper choice, *High Country News Books* has saved the following natural resources:

- 6.9 trees (40 feet in height)
- 2001 gallons water
- 1175 kwh electricity
- 17.1 pounds of air pollution

We are a member of Green Press Initiative—a nonprofit program supporting publishers in using fiber that is not sourced from ancient or endangered forests. For more information, visit www.greenpressinitiative.org.

FEED A FRIEND!

Receive two *FREE* issues of *High Country News*

High Country News is the only bi-weekly newspaper reporting on the West's natural resources, public lands, and changing communities. Covering 11 western states, from the Great Plains to the Northwest, and from the Northern Rockies to the desert Southwest, *High Country News* is an award-winning source for environmental news, analysis and commentary on water, logging, wildlife, grazing, wilderness, growth and other issues changing the face of the West.

To receive one free issue of *High Country News* and one for a friend, send your name and mailing address to:

HIGH COUNTRY NEWS
119 Grand Avenue
PO Box 1090
Paonia, CO 81428
1-800-905-1155 (phone)
970/527-4897 (fax)
circulation@hcn.org
www.hcn.org

THEN AGAIN, WHY WAIT?

If you don't want to wait to begin receiving the best reporting on the issues that most affect the American West, contact us using the information above to start your subscription immediately. And we have good news for your friend. Ask for our "Friend Subscription" and we'll discount your second subscription.